Mimetic Disillusion

Mimetic Disillusion

Eugene O'Neill, Tennessee Williams,
and U.S. Dramatic Realism

ANNE FLECHE

The University of Alabama Press

TUSCALOOSA AND LONDON

Excerpts from "The Rhetoric of Temporality," in *Blindness and Insight: Essays in the Rhetoric of Contemporary Criticism*, by Paul de Man, copyright © 1971 Oxford University Press, used by permission.

∞

The paper on which this book is printed meets the minimum requirements of American National Standard for Information Science–Permanence of Paper for Printed Library Materials, ANSI Z39.48-1984.

Library of Congress Cataloging-in-Publication Data

Fleche, Anne.
    Mimetic disillusion : Eugene O'Neill, Tennessee Williams, and U.S. dramatic realism / Anne Fleche.
       p.   cm.
    Includes bibliographical references and index.
    ISBN 0-8173-0838-5 (paper : alk. paper)
    1. American drama—20th century—History and criticism.
   2. O'Neill, Eugene, 1888–1953—Criticism and interpretation.
   3. Williams, Tennessee, 1911–1983—Criticism and interpretation.
   4. Realism in literature.   I. Title.
   PS338. R42F58   1997
   812′.5209—dc20   96-24510

British Library Cataloguing-in-Publication Data available

For Bets

Contents

Acknowledgments

I want to thank the people who read drafts of some or all of these chapters and offered their helpful suggestions: Thomas Van Laan, Thomas Edwards, Celeste Goodridge, Robin Lydenberg, and Eileen Sweeney. Scott Curtis and Lisa Cuklanz located the cover still. Elin Diamond has been my mimetic model, if not my icon; her sharp criticism and energetic support are a continuing inspiration. Love and thanks also to my mother and father, sisters and brothers, and thanks to my coworkers at Boston College, especially Patrice Scott who typed the manuscript, and my office-mate Bonnie Rudner who always provided comfort and support. Special thanks are long overdue to Laura Tanner, a patient, perceptive reader and a great friend. My sister Betsy Fleche has been my best pal and closest intellectual collaborator time out of mind. This book is for her.

Part of chapter 5 appears in slightly altered form as "The Space of Madness and Desire: Tennessee Williams and *Streetcar*," in *Modern Drama*, edited by David Blostein, Dorothy Parker, and Alan Thomas, copyright © 1995 by *Modern Drama*.

The line from "somewhere i have never travelled, gladly beyond" is reprinted from *Complete Poems: 1904–1962*, by E. E. Cummings, edited by George J. Firmage, by permission of Liveright Publishing Corporation. Copyright © 1931, 1959, 1991 by the Trustees for the E. E. Cummings Trust. Copyright © 1979 by George James Firmage.

Excerpts from *The Theater and Its Double*, by Antonin Artaud, translated by Mary Caroline Richards, copyright © 1958 by Grove Press, Inc. Used by permission.

Excerpts from *Brecht on Theatre: The Development of an Aesthetic*, edited and translated by John Willett, published by Methuen. Translation copyright © 1964 and renewed © 1992 by John Willett. Reprinted

Mimetic Disillusion

1 Introduction
Eugene O'Neill, Tennessee Williams, and U.S. Dramatic Theory, 1935–1947

> SHANNON: Yeah, well, you know we—live on two levels, Miss Jelkes, the realistic level and the fantastic level, and which is the real one, really. . . .
> HANNAH: I would say both, Mr. Shannon.
> SHANNON: But when you live on the fantastic level as I have lately but have got to operate on the realistic level, that's when you're spooked, that's the spook.

This exchange, from *The Night of the Iguana* (1961), by boldly undercutting its own illusionism as dialogue, imitates the very problem it appears to discuss. The disillusionment of Shannon, a former minister reduced to giving guided tours, presents him with the dilemma of the real/fantastic, which Hannah, the spiritual ("female") artist, represents as a false distinction: "I would say both." The "spook," or ghost or "double," of the real is inseparable from the scene of the real, and Hannah's answer, with its "both/and," offers no consoling duplicity.

Tennessee Williams's plays persistently question the relation of "art" to "reality," the problem of formal constraints in the theater, and the violence and destructiveness of closure, of establishing limits and defining moments. His plays create a language for these representational concepts: "real/fantastic," "fugitive," "deception," "transparent," "mendacity"; and visually he plays magic tricks that call attention to the theatrical illusion: he turns the set inside out and puts a Chinese lantern over the lightbulb. Perhaps it is this obsessive worrying over representation itself that makes Williams's dramas seem particularly unconcerned with getting anywhere and gives them their strong sense of undecidability and dislocation. Shannon's philosophical question to the muselike Miss Jelkes is not a real question any more than her reply is a real answer. But the

1

question really does *ask* something, and it is something the play really *cannot* answer. The measure of Williams's inventiveness as a playwright is his ability to think continually of new ways to reinvent the question.

"Metatheatre" might have been an answer, and in fact Williams's allegorical writing could have accommodated this theory of a theater-about-theater, thus sidestepping its relation to "reality" or at least putting it off. But Williams doesn't opt for it. He is still interested in what art has to do with "the real," even though, or perhaps because, as the similarly named Hannah and Shannon demonstrate, the distinction itself is part of the illusion. The presence of real people in the theater, responding to real systems of signification, however they interpret them, makes mimesis the crucial issue for anyone concerned with dramatic theory. A troubled term with various meanings—"copy," "imitation," "representation," "resemblance," "mimicry," etc.,[1] "mimesis" first acquires prominence in Greek philosophy with Plato, as Mihai Spariosu has shown (Spariosu III). Plato emphasizes the dangers of mimesis as fantastic rather than real in his plan to educate wise, reasonable philosopher kings for *The Republic*.[2] Mimesis as it first developed theoretically, then, is specifically identified with political ends and not with "pleasure" (also a complicated term for the Greeks).[3] The connection between drama and politics in the United States in the 1930s, which I will be discussing later in this chapter, is a particular moment in a long conceptual history. Aristotle is usually the classical model in this history of dramatic theory, and Brecht's influence is perhaps a good enough reason for this emphasis, but I want to begin by reexamining Plato's writings, since the Aristotle-Brecht connection gets much of the attention later on.

For Plato, dramatic poetry is especially dangerous because its form is so reliant upon multiplicity, mutability, and change—and judgments based on what changes are false. What Plato calls "representation" (mimesis) in drama, in fact, is *role-playing*: speeches in which one actually pretends to be somebody else. This mimesis he opposes to *narration*, a univocal or "lyric" mode. ("Epic," as with Brecht, employs both methods. See *The Republic*, 392cff.) The capacity for taking on different points of view is art's greatest danger and its chief limitation. Anyone who claims knowledge of many things (e.g., a playwright, who represents different kinds of people, good and bad) is for Plato really "a charlatan, whose apparent omniscience is due entirely to his own inability to distinguish knowledge, ignorance, and representation" (598d). The multiplicity of the point of view, and not "narration" (substituting pretense for authenticity), is the issue, as Plato has to admit, since he is narrating Socrates.

In the famous distinction between reality and illusion in book 10 of The Republic, the artist is said to imitate what the craftsman manufactures, the useful thing that is already at one remove from the higher reality of form. Furthermore, the artist can only imitate the particular thing from a particular point of view: "What I mean is this. If you look at a bed, or anything else, sideways or endways or from some other angle, does it make any difference to the bed? Isn't it merely that it *looks* different, without *being* different?" (598a). Indeed "all . . . representative artists" exploit optical effects contradictory to reason, placing art "in a fond liaison" with the less rational parts of the mind (603b). Painting, drama, and magic are for Plato equivalent activities: they go to bed with our instincts and dally with our perceptions.

Objects and representations of objects cannot lead us to truth; they are a dead end. To arrive at truth we must rely solely on reason (dialectic, discussion, philosophy), breaking down assumptions until we reach the forms, which are single and unified. Truth cannot be multiple, because it is the principle shared by two (or more) things (597c). It is what makes multiple things resemble each other. For Plato, then, reality is a mimetic circle of resemblances: everything reflects something else, since all ultimately reflect the forms. Passages from his late writings, such as The Laws and The Timaeus, reflect more directly upon The Republic's rather implicit dependence on this notion, perhaps because these books are specifically about the processes of organization and creation (respectively).

For example, in The Laws, Plato suggests that representation (mimesis) is the law that replicates itself throughout human endeavor—in fact it is the law that specifically links art and the state. What is most important in art is accuracy, the correct reproduction of the model (668); similarly, the state is "a 'representation' of the finest and noblest life—the very thing we maintain is most genuinely a tragedy. So we are poets like yourselves, composing in the same genre, and your competitors as artists and actors in the finest drama, which true law alone has the natural power to 'produce' to perfection (of that we're quite confident)" (817). In *The Laws* Plato's awareness of the dialogue's self-reflexivity is underscored, as it is in the passage above, again and again. "An Athenian Stranger," for example, takes the usual place of Socrates as teacher/narrator, and he makes explicit references to the textuality of his speeches, aware that he is producing a literary work to be used as instruction (and even in *The Republic* Plato had argued that some literature could be instructive).

> You see, when I look back now over this discussion of ours, . . . well, it's come to look, to my eyes, just like a literary composition. Perhaps not surprisingly, I was overcome by a feeling of immense satisfaction at the sight of my "collected works," so to speak, because, of all the addresses I have ever learned or listened to, whether in verse or in this kind of free prose style I've been using, it's *these* that have impressed me as being the most eminently acceptable and the most entirely appropriate for the ears of the younger generation. [*The Laws* 811]

In setting down *The Laws*, the model to be copied, then, Plato recognizes the "stranger" in himself, the uncanniness of the writer, who opens the door into the very realm of repetition from which he flees. The disguise of literary composition enables him to speak, but from a position Plato humorously undercuts as suspect, presumptuous, unconvincing. He likens his writing to tragedy (because both are morally serious) in self-deprecating terms. And he seems wittily aware of his reliance on language and metaphor.[4] As long as we are in a world of images—visual or verbal—we are inside a perfect mimetic model, playing with a complete set of perfectly mimetic figures or copies that cannot move beyond their self-reflexivity. (Partly, the reason is that the copies are contained in space, which is the position or receptacle of reality. Space must always be the same because it is capable of receiving anything—see, e.g., *The Timaeus* 29–53.)

When Plato is on the verge of describing the antithesis of mimesis, namely truth itself, he stops: "because what you'd see would no longer be an image of what we are talking about but the truth itself, that is, as I see it; one ought not at this point to claim certainty, though one can claim that there is something of the kind to see, don't you think?" (*The Republic* 533a). The pervasiveness of images, of language and of what Aristotle, speaking of drama, calls "thought" ("all the effects that have to be produced by means of language"—*On the Art of Poetry* 57–58), is something Plato faces head-on, and it's why he thinks we should just *control art* (the poet is *out of control*—cf. *The Laws* 719). Yet on the other hand, as his addition of "space" to the Form/Copy dyad in *The Timaeus* seems to suggest, for Plato art orders the mess and chaos of life. It names and locates. So, as Oscar Wilde said, life imitates art, tries to shape and organize and possess itself. This notion isn't the reverse of censorship but its obverse; Wilde's aestheticism isn't abandonment but another version of mimetic control.[5] And beneath both ideas, Plato's and Wilde's, lies a perception or perhaps even a fear of chaos and a desire to close the mimetic circle against it. Thus for Plato as well as Aristotle, mimesis is fundamental, a tautology.

In *The Timaeus* there is at least the theoretical possibility that language could be true and not metaphorical, but only relatively, "as irrefutable and uncontrovertible as a description in words can be"; but "both I and you . . . are merely human, and should not look for anything more than a likely story in such matters" (29). As long as it is about *change* (the world, the universe, human life), language will be inaccurate, stuck in the holding pattern of meaning, "a likely story."

For Aristotle, change could be positive—it was no longer, as it was for Plato, the very model of falseness. Aristotle's idea was that change needn't result in endless replication but could represent an evolutionary motion toward an end. We can learn from mistakes and contingencies as well as from virtue—"real" or "imitated."[6] The limitation of art, its point of view, is exactly Aristotle's point of departure for the mimetic theory with which he has been credited;[7] in Aristotle we find the seeds of Plato. The mighty influence of Platonic philosophy on Western artistic theory has perhaps all along been mediated by Aristotle's mimetic glass, and there has been something suspicious in our reliance on Plato as a source for the truth/illusion binary. (This binary is inherent, in fact, in the Greek language, since "Aletheia," the Greek word for "truth," means " 'what is revealed,' 'what is brought out from concealment' " [Nussbaum 241].) Brecht seems to suggest something about Aristotle's primary influence, for Aristotle, the sometime villain of Brechtian theater, is really much more useful to Brecht than that implies. Brecht consciously writes Aristotle into new being, as a collaborator in modern theater's critical confrontation with representational principles. Aristotle writes the other half of Brecht's "antimimetic" theory—or rather, Brecht (very platonically) *narrates* Aristotle, pretending, half of the time, to be Aristotle.[8]

But there is yet another possible use for "mimesis," a less familiar one, because it is less explicitly connected to politics and morality. Mihai Spariosu has developed a notion of pre-Platonic "mimetic" "play" that is presentational rather than representational, though both are related, he says, to a "power principle lying at the foundation of Western civilization" (III).[9] This "nonmimetic" or "Dionysian" play Spariosu describes as a "turn[ing] away from history, without taking refuge in the eternal," "the end of Western civilization as we know it at present" (101). Spariosu criticizes the French philosopher Jacques Derrida for his play with mimesis, which subverts the unifying principle at the heart of Plato's philosophy while retaining its play of surfaces, because Derrida continues to discuss play in relation to metaphysics (78–79). "There should no longer be a question of displacing or overcoming, but rather one of turning away, of 'digressing' *without* 'transgressing' " (79). Derrida, Spariosu argues, leaves the "power-principle" intact, as his appropriation by certain colonial academies would suggest: "This is particularly evident in American academia, where poststructuralism has taken the form of an *ideology*, replacing New Criticism and approaching what Edward Said calls a 'new orthodoxy' " (79).

While I don't want to minimize the role of the academy in power relations, of various kinds and degrees, it seems to me that Spariosu's notion of power is disingenuous. After all, academia is often attacked as a source of political hegemony, as a kind of referent or substitute for political administrations, whose control of rhetoric and media is, one would think, more clearly demonstrable. And language and interpretation continue to be the language and interpretation of power, whether they refer to history (i.e., for Spariosu, the history of Western civilization, hence metaphysics) or "turn away from it."

The notion of "turning," or "digressing," does not avoid defining history by seeking to avoid it.

More important, Elin Diamond, among others, has argued that relations of power are inherent in the mimetic sign-referent exchange. And so we cannot speak of power, or even identify what it is we want to avoid about it, outside the play of referents.[10] Moreover, Diamond, who as a feminist is perhaps more conscious of the important symbolic power of taking a position than is Spariosu, recognizes (like Plato) that in writing her essay she assumes a certain relation to the truth, "however provisional":

> Feminists, in our different constituencies, with our different objects of analysis, seek to intervene in the symbolic systems—linguistic, theatrical, political, psychological—and intervention requires assuming a subject position, however provisional, and making truth claims, however flexible, concerning one's own representations. [59]

The classical Western tradition has tied up its dramatic criticism in the struggle between politics and art. (Sometimes politics is also called "morality" or "usefulness," and similarly art, when it is not politically or morally "good," is called something else—"pornography," "propaganda," "popular culture.") "There is," as Plato remarks in *The Republic*, "an old quarrel between philosophy and poetry" (607b). And artistic changes do in fact seem to indicate shifts in the social/political atmosphere: an alteration in style presupposes an alteration in the way the audience is perceived.[11] It is probably naive to think that we can think of art apart from politics.[12] And this is especially true of the drama, where, as in film, a large collaborative effort is required for production.

There has been renewed interest in the problem of mimesis, at least since World War II, occasioned perhaps as much by political changes as anything else. At least, the debate has, as Diamond's remarks suggest, seemed to create antagonisms over political questions of activism and social efficacy. The question asked by Harry Levin in 1951, "What Is Realism?" was a timely one, given the recent works of realistic investigation by O'Neill and Williams that I explore in the following chapters, and it is still a central question in literary—and especially dramatic—theory. At the time Levin did not see realism as an unmixed form, nor did he think its formal assumptions durable. Identifying the perception of realism with its practice, Levin saw it as a bourgeois art that couldn't sustain its assumptions. Partly, Levin was right: realism, as its name implies, inevitably falls short of its goal, pointing to a fullness beyond itself that is representation's seductive power and its limitation. And Levin was hardly speaking of some "naive" realism that couldn't envision change; on the contrary, the mix of "convention" and "realism" he saw in the writing of that time Levin described as itself "transitional": realistic art contains the means for liberation from its own conventional rigidity, because realists tend to "transcend their own class, to criticize the bourgeoisie" (199).

But to those who see realism as itself freighted with convention, its persistence into the latter half of the century suggests deeper affinities with dramatic conception. Its self-contradictoriness has in retrospect seemed not transitional but radical, fundamental, pointing directly to the mimetic dilemma: how can the representation of the truth not betray itself? Levin gives realistic writers a lot of credit in suggesting that they inevitably transcend their class blinders as they become more and more self-critical: he attributes to them, in fact, a philosophy. It's no accident that Plato was the first Western writer to pose the question of realism and representation in the drama; for the practical questions about representation are also philosophical: what can we perceive, and how do we perceive it, and what do we mean when we assign meaning to what we perceive?

That a metaphysical criticism can or needs to be done of what we have been calling "realism" is certainly not self-evident: to a certain rational observer the inquiry into realism will appear as fraud—or, worse, as lazy: an attack on the weak and defenseless, the dead, the passé. One might observe that such a view positions itself on high ground, looking from the station or present back upon obscure beginnings and forward toward the successful culmination of self-transcendence. But "history" is a "past" that keeps on the move: the appearance of temporal disparity can be misleading, the recovery of sequence an endless task. The realistic bias may not be ready to be relegated simply to "history," especially as "history" in this sense is far too complacent.[13] Any investigation of realism—like realistic art itself—has to start from the belief that it is necessary to examine the necessary or obvious, to question the true; for "representational" art is a self-contradictory thing, pointing toward its promised reality, never arriving at it. The critic, like the artist, must continually reconstruct the reality she is questioning, testing the possibilities for meaning of the most obvious mental furniture. Representation isn't after all something that makes the critic innocent and the art guilty —it doesn't detour criticism. Brecht writes for (vor) Aristotle somehow, as Plato dictates to Socrates.[14] The critic of course is representing continually: nothing has arrived until the critic sends it. Her assertions are always guilty assertions, catching at things until they get caught. And while there is guilt there is life—Aristotle and Plato are messily, disturbingly alive in the criticism that starts by assuming they are dead.

With such assertions to make I have not hesitated to address the current literary debate over realism through the writings of dramatists no longer extant—indeed, writers widely regarded as dead in more ways than one. From the standpoints of criticism and production, death came too early for O'Neill, too late for Williams. O'Neill's career at present rests on posthumous plays (*Long Day's Journey into Night*) and posthumous revivals (such as the 1956 production of *The Iceman Cometh*); while about half of Williams's career—in his case the latter half—remains in limbo, mostly unread, unacknowledged, unproduced. The two writers' careers overlap in the World War II period, when they composed the plays studied in this book, those written between 1939 (*The Iceman Cometh*) and 1947 (*A Streetcar Named Desire*). These are the plays they are remembered for, the plays that have influenced the generation since the war, and it may seem, fifty years later, that nothing has been left unsaid about them—except what couldn't have been said, in this way, until now.

In retrospect the period of the forties is important for U.S. drama, marking a transition between the dramatic realistic renaissance of the thirties and its aftermath. This period marks the threshold between a lower-middle-class play like Odets's *Awake and Sing!* (1935) and Williams's *The Glass Menagerie* (1944), another family drama set in an urban apartment that seems wholly different. Or consider the threshold between the urban barroom plays, such as Saroyan's wish-fulfillment fantasy *The Time of Your Life*, and O'Neill's devastating *The*

Iceman Cometh, both written in 1939. It's difficult to describe whatever transition is taking place here, impossible to localize it or date it, but in general the move was to put the thirties into the past and to put the present into some vague otherwhere, from which everything took on the distance of memory, framed with a kind of painful arbitrariness, unreachable yet obsessively desired. What happens in the family apartment or the crummy bar shifts palpably to what doesn't happen, what can be done to what can be imagined or talked about. A confidence in the future approaching swagger becomes the crushing burden of memory (the temporal "movement" of the play being exactly reversed). Maybe Joe in *The Time of Your Life* is a transitional figure: he plans things, but he never actually does anything himself. In a climactic moment, he stands on the threshold of the bar, pointing a gun out the door, and for a moment he looks like he's shooting someone—but a moment later, it seems the gun hasn't gone off.

The long, troubled history of U.S. dramatic realism in the nineteenth and early twentieth centuries might conveniently be telescoped into the 1930s, when realism's ideological assumptions were exploited (and so tested) by a new socially conscious generation of playwrights. Once again, as in Ibsen's day, realistic drama was the preferred form for re-form, and like Ibsen's imitators, thirties playwrights found that realistic drama was also the "popular" drama that would reach large and diverse audiences. The influence of "social" urgency and "socialist" doctrine in the thirties had resulted in a version of realistic drama that addressed itself to socioeconomic problems specifically; it called working- and middle-class spectators to action for a better future. Yet to be commercially successful it was still very close to the nineteenth-century "bourgeois" realism whose complacency it attacked. John Howard Lawson was the most influential communist dramatic theorist in the United States; his book *Theory and Technique of Playwriting* (1936), praised by the left-wing critic John Gassner as "the most incisive and illuminating treatment of playwriting as a dynamic art," shows how close socialist or revolutionary realism came to left-wing social realism (sometimes called "Moral" or "reform" drama)[15] and how much socialist realism leaned upon nineteenth-century realism and classical theory. Lawson's socialist realism sounds mostly antisymbolist:

Socialist realism is opposed to either a subjective or a naturalistic method: the artist cannot be content with an impression or with superficial appearances—with fragments and odds and ends of reality. He must find the inner meaning of events; but there is nothing *spiritual* about this inner meaning; it is not subjective and is not a reflection of the moods and passions of the soul; the inner meaning of events is revealed by discovering the *real* connections of cause and effect which underlie the events; the artist must condense these causes; he must give them their proper color and proportion and quality; he must dramatize the "superstructure of diversified and characteristic sentiments, illusions, habits of thought, and outlooks on life in general." [Lawson 47–48, italics in the original; Lawson is quoting Marx]

Lawson's dramatic theory, as his language suggests, is more than faintly Aristotelian ("proper color and proportion and quality"), and as Ira Levine points out, it is "realistic" in the nineteenth-century bourgeois sense, since it relies on causal structure, scène-à-faire, and climax: "Clearly, this structure was derived from the construction of the nineteenth-century 'well-made' play, upon which the structure of bourgeois realistic drama had been based" (127). Even more revealing (and confusing) perhaps is the fact that "Only one contemporary critic (Wiegand) noticed this anachronism" (ibid.). Realism's durability as a formal structure helps in a way to explain both its theoretical contradictoriness and its historical indiscrimination.

In fact four years before Lawson's book, Philip Rahv had theorized a revolutionary notion of "catharsis," one that, unlike Aristotle's "static, passive conception quite in line with the needs of a slave-owning class," would incite the spectator to action, instead of leaving him or her "limp and reconciled to the 'immutable laws of life' " (Rahv, quoted in Levine 124). "A proletarian drama, for instance, inspires a spectator with pity as he identifies himself with the characters on the stage; he is terror-stricken by the horror of the worker's existence under capitalism; but these two emotions [are] finally fused in the white heat of battle into a revolutionary deed" (ibid.; alterations Levine's).

Besides bringing socialist realism into a telling closeness with classical mimetic theory, Rahv's concept of "revolutionary catharsis" well expresses the powerful sense in socialist realism that the drama must be a call to action, not a pacifying entertainment.[16] Lawson too stresses the active will of the protagonist, developing a theory proposed by Ferdinand Brunetière ("The Law of the Drama," 1894, trans. 1914); "Brunetière held that fatalism makes drama impossible; drama lies in man's attempt to dominate his surroundings" (Lawson 59). Tragic or despairing plays suggested that the world was static, that change was impossible, and they reconciled the spectator to the social status quo. Given this notion it is easy to see how critical aversion could arise to plays of " 'the Eugene O'Neill bourgeois reactionary variety, in which the audience is asked to weep over the sexual problems of a finance-capitalist swindler' " ("Success Story," *Daily Worker*, October 3, 1932, 1, no author given; quoted in Himelstein 161). Of course a "naturalistic" play like Jack Kirkland's *Tobacco Road* (1933) was criticized by the Left as too pessimistic ("it portrayed man as a victim of a mechanistic world unresponsive to social action"—Levine 112); and in his 1960 introduction to *Theory and Technique of Playwriting*, Lawson, writing of Tennessee Williams, marvels that "the themes of guilt and lost identity, criminal impulses and profitless despair, evoke an emotional response in the American audience" (xvi); "Williams' pessimism is visceral and mindless" (xviii).

It seems that O'Neill and Williams stand apart from the realistic renaissance of the thirties, but where they stand is unclear. Their reaction against realism is nonetheless a response to real conditions of representation, and both writers seem aware that the conditions of representation are not socially irrelevant. Though they aren't accepted by socialist realist theorists, O'Neill and Williams seem still to straddle some line of division between thirties realism and a philosophical rejection of it. O'Neill, for example, attacks U.S. capitalist greed and its cycle of exploitation and despair, particularly in his cycles *Mourning Becomes Electra* (1931) and the unfinished "Tale of Possessors Self Dispossessed" (ca. 1935–). But he is not recognized as a socially significant writer, any more than Williams, although both write about realistic settings and character types. *Long Day's Journey into Night* and *A Streetcar Named Desire* are frequently categorized as realistic, even naturalistic, and produced in realistic style, yet compared with the realism around them (Arthur Miller's, e.g.), they exhibit far less faith in the social efficacy of art. The dramas of O'Neill and Williams take realism in a different direction—less obvious, more self-critical. Ibsen, Chekhov, Shaw—all had shown the way out of realism's binding "truth" by exploring the conventions of its representation; yet at the end of the 1930s U.S. dramatists had to address the problem again, in a new era of social programs, global war, and a consciously politicized theater.

That thirties socialist realism felt at home with Aristotelian poetics isn't surprising. Aristotle's definition of drama—"a thing done" —as the representation of an *action* presumes a representable world of change, human activity, intervention, and development. He makes art part of a process, a means to an end, that is itself action: "The purpose of living is an end which is a kind of activity, not a quality; . . . [A]nd as always, the end is everything" (*On the Art of Poetry* 39–40). This is why plotting is the most important part of tragedy, for Aristotle. It is that which enacts the change, the "action and life," "happiness and unhappiness" that tragedy represents (39). And *because* it is about action it is also about *persons*.

This view of the structure of a single tragedy as a process is mimicked in the development of tragedy as a genre. "Little by little tragedy advanced, each new element being developed as it came into use, until after many changes it attained its natural form and came to a standstill" (36). Aristotle's organicism, while it admits development and change and gives primary place to action—all vital to a poetics of politically conscious art—nevertheless envisions a completion of this process, a telos or end, though easily mistaken and not easily defined (cf. *Politics* 1339b10–39b31, 1337b33–38a13), beyond which we cannot even look, let alone see. So in the great push to arrive at our natural form, and wondering whether we've gotten there or whether this is just another stage of becoming, we must remember that there is something that we are supposed to be, all along. The answer to the riddle, the conclusion of the plot, is final, inevitable—and hidden, elsewhere.

Aristotle's politics judges actions by their effects, justifies actions on the grounds of a theoretical end, and presumes the evolutionary rightness of change. In *Politics* Aristotle argues for the unifying principle of the natural through a series of mirror effects: the individual, created through the association of a male and female, associates with others to form households, villages, a state; and each part stands for the whole (1331b24–31b39, 1337a11–37a33). So while Aristotle may seem democratically to include many things in his philosophy—inconsistency, ambiguity, the material conditions of an act (*On the Art of Poetry* 71–72ff.), the effect they create must finally be one of symmetry.[17] In the end, inconsistency, incommensurability, and irrationality or perverseness are scandalous, censored (*On the Art of Poetry* 74 and cf. *The Republic* 346 n. 2). For Aristotle as for Plato, then, symmetry is effectively defined and controlled by politics, because human beings live to organize politically, and therefore a political organism in small is what a human being is: "for whatever is the end-product of the coming into existence of any object, that is what we call its nature" (*Politics*, 1252b27).

Left-wing dramatic theory in the thirties thus found it useful to argue in Aristotelian terms. Popular Front tactics were themselves an Aristotelian middle way to attract a wider audience to left-wing plays (Levine 133), adjusting means to achieve a desired end. But political events in the United States after 1938 must have indicated to these writers that the natural Aristotelian connection between means and ends was not in fact the order of things and that perhaps it was time to rethink art's relationship to reality in less optimistic terms. The anti-Communist witch-hunt, the anti–New Deal backlash, and the effects of the developing war in Europe had devastating and depressing effects on left-wing theater.[18]

Certainly U.S. drama since the end of the thirties has never been "socialist" again. The belief in action for a better future has largely gone out of realism, making the thirties dramas sound older than they are. (Many of them survive in the popular mind only through the patina of Hollywood film nostalgia, and these are the plays with a soft enough radicalism to sell as films.) Though postthirties drama is still, as John Gassner has pointed out (11–14), mainly "realistic" in style, it no longer focuses hopefully on analyses of and solutions to social problems. (That has become the work of television movies.) For their part, O'Neill and Williams seem especially to struggle with realistic form in the wake of the thirties, to see its philosophical problems and conceptual ironies during the formal and ideological changes of the war years. Perhaps as a consequence, they are accused by their critics, and even by some of their friends, of having big intentions, or disgusting ones, of being fatalistic, pessimistic, self-interested, or self-indulgent—criticisms that often sound like leftover left-wing commentary from the thirties, New Criticism's partisan reviews. Williams in particular has been singled out for derision, but most of O'Neill's plays, as the centenary reminded us, are seldom produced. So as dramatic theory revisits mimesis, it looks as though Williams and O'Neill deserve a fresh look.

In the United States, for the last twenty years at least, the central figure in the reevaluation of Platonic, real/fantastic, representational theory has been Jacques Derrida.[19] The introduction of French poststructuralism to the U.S. academy has spurred new analyses of mimesis, and its theorists have been strongly associated with the question of mimesis in contemporary debates.[20] Yet as most of the writing, past and present, on mimesis has shown, the word refers not only to artistic practice but also to art's reception: mimesis is above all a way of reading and perceiving, since it concerns not only resemblance but its underlying assumption of presence. The from-where-one-looks recedes continually from view.[21] Similarly "representation" isn't limited by requirements of "photographic realism" but extends equally toward the relative and the relational—toward what is or may be perceived as a like or an equivalent. "Realism," which in dramatic circles commonly tends to become the focal term of debate rather than "mimesis," is more theoretically useful in its slipperiness than in any strict sense, as a set of assumptions with which to construct or read or watch a play. Yet the word "realism" contains within its significance concerns of copy, resemblance, and social relations summarized by "mimesis." "Realism" is in fact the only theatrical term that achieves this mimetic fullness of reference.

Not coincidentally, then, realism has remained the dominant philosophical basis of modern and contemporary drama.[22] Its commodiousness and flexibility as a term have at times masked or complicated its claims to verifiable "truth," but realism continues to carry the day as well as the greatest weight of mimetic information. And yet, considering the attention spent on representation and the Platonic real/ideal since the 1960s by philosophers interested in splitting such apparently unsplittable binaries, dramatic literature has gotten surprisingly scant notice. Derrida, at least, seems interested in dramatic theory. His essays on Artaud in *Writing and Difference* (*L'écriture et la différence*, 1967) explore the painful separation of the "theatre" from its "double" though without quite acknowledging where such a notion of "theatre" might lead. In the essay "La parole soufflée," Derrida is wisely reluctant to make a case of, or for, Artaud, staying with the "spirit" of Artaud's thorough confrontation with metaphysics (194), and in "The Theater of Cruelty and the Closure of Repetition," there is presumably no theater without repetition, representation: "Artaud . . . desired the impossibility of the theater" (249). We can "think of the closure of representation," "conceive of the closure of that [i.e., representation] which is without end" (250), but we cannot make a theater of this theory. Derrida leaves us at the beginning (again) of a new deconstructive project in *Writing and Difference*.

Five years later, however, Derrida returned to the question of theatrical representation. In "The Double Session," he proposes that Mallarmé's "Mimique," as an imitation that, rather than reflecting reality, "produces reality-effects," is "mimesis" without the Platonic reference to truth (*Dissemination* 206). Moreover, such a mimesis is only possible as a " 'perpetual allusion,' "—that is, a kind of mise en abyme of textual citation. "Mimique" "copies" that which has never existed and never will exist. This reading of "Mimique" is not, however, Derrida suggests, a new idealism but a continual displacement of priorities, a continual opening of possible readings.

Derrida's allusive mimesis is perhaps most visible in the plays of Jean Genet, where race and gender are relentlessly reread through theatrical gesture, costume, pose, nuance, and so forth. Indeed, Judith Butler has argued via Derrida for a notion of gender as imitation, as what is assumed through repetitive acts of gender citation. Derrida and Butler thus theorize the necessary absence of a "real" or "true" that is approximated by representation (mimesis). Such imitations, however, continually produce the phantom of a prior truth as the effect of representation and consequently require an ongoing interpretive effort to undo them. In "The Double Session" Derrida has undone the impasse of representation yet again, and in so doing he has moved the discussion of mimesis from the level of the theatrical apparatus to the level of the subject and agency, where Butler takes it up.

That "Mimique," as Derrida shows, perpetually displaces the sequence of priorities—of model and copy, idea and imitation—demonstrates a playful urge in the theater (playfully deferred) to get (back) to an origin, imagined as an extra- or a pretheatrical event, an invisibility prior to representation. The invisible, the undramatizable, is the limit *toward* which the theatrical looks ("theater" and "theory" sharing the same Latin root "thea," "act of seeing").[23] The mimetic property of theater, then, the law that seems to stand implacably behind it, should be the object of analysis and not the theater as it is presumed to exist or in its present possibilities for existence. Theater, however, provides the best conditions for such an analysis: historically, classically, practically, theater is the central genre for the mimetic inquiry. As Derrida says of Artaud, theater was, for him, *the* genre, since "theater summons the totality of existence and no longer tolerates either the incidence of interpretation or the distinction between actor and author. The initial urgent requirement of an in-organic theater is emancipation from the text" (187). In drama the process of signification leaps into view. We can watch it covering its tracks on different levels of perception: the written/spoken word, the visible/implied space, the utilitarian/symbolic object, the particular/typical human being, and the synchronization of sound and gesture. As Derrida notes, drama directly affronts the primacy of the text, crossing it out by crossing over it in self-conscious rehearsals (repetitions) for the completion—that is, the presence—of the "text." In order to create Artaudian theater, a theater that is not (a) double, the text has to be "resituated" farther down the line: it can no longer occupy, in the sense of preoccupy, the theater.

[Artaud] will only attempt the resituation and subordination of speech—the until now enormous, pervasive, ubiquitous, bloated speech [*parole soufflée*] which had exorbitantly weighed upon theatrical space. . . . And the syntax governing the succession of word gestures will no longer be a grammar of predication, a logic of "clear thinking" or of a knowing consciousness. [188]

Artaud is, of course, after nothing *less* than a totalizing experience of "theater," a deep "communion" (see Esslin, 75–76) among "actors" and "audience" that will transcend the verbal logic on which Western theater is based. But truly to reoccupy the place of speech, the ultimate, the true place of theater, requires a painful evacuation of the material of consciousness—in other words, a retention of the work, in order that speech and gesture no longer speak and gesture for the work, the logic or "grammar of predication" that drives all before it (188; the scatological language in reference to the "work," as Derrida shows, is very marked in Artaud's writings). To say, then, that a dramatic "text" does not consist (merely) of "words" side-steps the problem of text itself, the idea of a text, or a theater, which precedes such a statement. Even Artaud, as Derrida and others have said, does not obliterate text and verbal text at one blow. Artaud seems to see that it is more a question of obliterating the writer, author, authority Him/Itself. The text is small change by comparison.

One small step in Artaud's direction is the undermining of the text's revelatory status, particularly its status as revelation of a single authorial declamation or position. In order to do this, the text cannot be seen, obviously, to "reveal" anything, not even its own failure to reveal. In other words, metatheatre—a self-consciousness of its form—does not go far enough. Since it mimes its own function, metatheatre imitates or doubles the revelatory process at the level of aesthetics. It imitates art. This practice is subversion, but it is not capable of further subversion. Double-crossing the text, it covers old ground. Metatheatre, at its best, displaces the theater only to reinstall it at a higher level of abstraction. It looks down as if scornfully at the very problem it would seem to solve. I think we have to look for texts that work through mimetic possibilities rather than replicating or doubling them.

Eugene O'Neill's and Tennessee Williams's texts are not only amenable to poststructuralist readings; they are, I think, part of the age of poststructuralist thinking that has grown up since the war and has taken such hold in U.S. criticism. Their most "classic" and "characteristic" texts—the famous ones, studied in this book—are much harder to *read*, logically, dramatically, as texts, than the proliferating scholarship around them might lead one to expect. And these plays are, as I will show, most difficult and therefore interesting, to read as expressions of mimetic and realist theories of drama. Yet Williams and O'Neill—who might otherwise seem unlikely cohabitants of a single study—continually *refer to* the referential bias of theater and in so doing call it into question. In order to criticize realistic/mimetic biases, both writers seriously invoke them, not to subsume them in metatheatre's self-referentiality, but to face the deep power of their assumptions. In this process they understand that their theater and theory "must inhabit the structures they demolish" (*Writing and Difference* 194). So although *The Iceman Cometh* and *A Streetcar Named Desire*, say, are not stylistically "realistic," they are deeply knowing about realistic style and about its underlying philosophy.

The plays in this study are not in chronological order; they do not build to a climax. I do, however, begin with the mimetic implications of speech and character, in *Long Day's Journey into Night*, investigating the notion of the text as the subversion of the primacy of speech, as revelatory urtext, as mutually reinforced by mise-en-scène, as defining of parameters of "character." This investigation of textual priority, as I have shown, lies at the heart of mimetic theory and its tradition in the West. The different categories common (in my view) to realism (and thus mimesis) that I examine in these chapters cannot really be separated from this tradition. Aristotle's emphasis on plot, time, character, memory, anterior action, speech, and so forth are most difficult to ignore, not as aesthetic guidelines for theatrical production, but as terms of knowledge and identity; they span that chasm in which representation and reality mingle and mesh. For this reason realism, as both a style and a theory, has been consistently *before* every modern dramatist and playgoer and accommodating to changes in perceptions about self and world.[24] And for this reason too realism seems powerfully tied to a pseudoreligious or ritual "past" as well as to a political material empirical "present." (Arguably the tension between these poles defines the mood—and the mode—of "modernism.") The Greeks' problem of connecting art with ethics, or morality, is still a problem, because the theater presents "action," as Aristotle called it, in the terms of character, time, and space, as a spectacle in which memory and immediacy act out their codependency.

I have also focused upon O'Neill and textuality (language, character, coherence, etc.), first, because O'Neill's counterrealism seems more language- and text-based than Williams's. Indeed, O'Neill had difficulties with production because he wrote so much; he exploded the confines of dramatic textual—and hence temporal—limitations. (The logical connection between chapters 2 and 3 lies just in this relation of textuality to temporality.) Like Hauptmann, whose ultradetailed realism he admired, O'Neill is a kind of stage novelist, a playwright who writes books.[25] In their detail and duration O'Neill's plays hold up well in the reading, while production conventions may seem to stifle or belittle them. His drama is as entwined with textual and readerly concerns as novels are, and these first chapters on O'Neill will seem, ideally, as relevant to the student of prose fiction as to the student of drama.

In *Long Day's Journey into Night*, a family tries to discuss its problems and reveal its feelings about them, but it keeps going over and over the same ground, until what in a realistic drama ought to have been simply exposition becomes a complex shifting mass of deniable "facts" and ambivalent emotions. Ultimately, at the end of a very long, very talky play, there is still no consensus on a place to begin, no synchronized moment when the characters inhabit the same history. Without this grounding the tussle of wills is soon unbearably stretched out, taut: this play defines suspense.

The Iceman Cometh, the next play addressed in the book, steps out of the family into a social—an international—historical world, specifically to question time's promise: of arrival, culmination, fulfillment, and meaning. Having a place in history seems to require each character to stand at an imaginary point looking backward and forward (into a past and future that amount to the same thing) and never entering time at all. To enter time is to destroy the imaginary ground on which the character is supported; it pulls the foundation out from under him, and he "falls" into reality as into the void, losing the identifying characteristics possible through his ironic detachment from history—losing in fact any ability to *see* history once he is firmly inside it.[26] Chapters 2 and 3, then, on O'Neill, remain inside the problem of textuality itself, the mimetic question of writing and reality, which has its implications not only for drama and the novel but also for the "likely story" of history. And this focus seems appropriate for O'Neill, not only because his plays invoke it, but also because of his own powerful presence (which by the time he composed these plays he very well knew) as father figure and originator of, and preeminent influence upon, "American" drama.

Williams is another case. He triumphantly enters the U.S. dramatic scene in the late period of O'Neill's silence (in production), eclipse, and relative inappreciation. (The late plays produced in O'Neill's lifetime, notably The Iceman Cometh, were not received as well in the forties as they were a decade later.) Hence, there was nobody in Williams's way as a playwright, and his early works received particular attention. Williams began his career in an era of scenic innovations in the theater, and The Glass Menagerie immediately makes use of elaborate lighting and translucent scenery (though his original stage directions are seldom used). Williams's early plays then, represented in this study, are the work of a young playwright, of a younger generation than O'Neill's.

The difference in approach to materials and métier is striking. Williams's verbal text is lighter and looser, in general, than O'Neill's and less discursive. And visually he breaks radically with speech. As the text grows lighter, less novelistic than verselike, the stage becomes a flexible play of light and shade, and it is colorful, "dramatic." The hints in O'Neill's staging that mise-en-scène was itself a language to be reckoned with are in Williams already a lexicon, full of expressive tints and faint mnemonic rumblings, never representational. One of the most persistent critical statements about Williams is his concern with time, but you look at the stage space, not your watch, to know what time it is in theater, and Williams knows that time begins when things are created in space.[27] And time is measured in relation to space: one's position is all important, and positioning in space is as crucial as positioning in time (and so in the creation of theoretical positions, interpretations). My studies of The Glass Menagerie and A Streetcar Named Desire thus look from the perceptual changes in space, in these plays, in order to visualize what space means to their construction. This is already a somewhat unusual point of departure for a drama critic, and my criticism of Williams may seem more abstractly or less conventionally centered than the chapters on O'Neill. Thus the Williams chapters have been placed later than the O'Neill chapters, as if moving from the relatively familiar to the relatively strange.

In fact the question of space is not secondary to the question of language in the theory of the theater—is not, really, a separate question at all but only seems so. For if, as Derrida suggests, speech has been, all along, weighing on theatrical space, the burden of language is born(e) in space; and if this burden is at all lifted, space will rise up in its own voice. In order to develop a theory of space in the drama (and here I should remind the reader that *The Glass Menagerie* and *A Streetcar Named Desire*—like the other plays in this book—were written for the proscenium stage), I have accented the two Williams chapters differently. Chapter 4 sets up some of the conditions of viewing into and through space on the stage, using Brechtian theory and film aesthetics, especially, to illustrate the filmic, changing perspectives in *The Glass Menagerie*. The tenement in St. Louis, with all its aesthetic and spatial limitations, is continually transformed into attenuated images, perceptual expansions. The very walls of the rooms turn out to be curtains whose practical function exposes their theoretical one: to show us where to look and what is "revealed." Chapter 5, on *A Streetcar Named Desire*, considers more fully the allegorical uses of space. In *Streetcar*'s violent nocturnal images, vision and not scenery makes places, sets boundaries, liberates and imprisons. Particularly in the scene in which Stanley rapes Blanche, the possibilities for stage lighting and sound to interpret words and gestures are exposed and heightened. The play's "climax" looks like an apocalypse, to which its anticlimactic ending scene seems wholly inadequate, incommensurate with *Streetcar*'s visionary excesses. In the end, the reassurances of form are anything but reassuring: they seem like violence, themselves, like the suppression of something that urgently needs to be expressed.

The major influence on both Williams chapters, however—as will be evident—is Michel Foucault, whose careful attention to and avoidance of the exclusionary tactics of sexual and social logic make him Williams's strong ally. In *The History of Sexuality, Volume 1, Discipline and Punish, Madness and Civilization*, and elsewhere, Foucault explores the institutionalization of Truth and the social structures—literal and philosophical—that constrain thought and expression. By starting from the premise that these structures of meaning and value are historical, developed over time, in response to social pressures, Foucault is able to give certain "realistic" and "rational" ideological lines the slip. He rebuilds the organizational principles of social reality from the ground up, making them no longer shadowy and complacent but surprising, visible, capable of their own logic. Foucault's writings provide sight lines for the deviance Williams improvises; in Streetcar, especially, Williams's destabilization of referents and of focal points has a poststructural rigor that doesn't bear scrutiny within the conventions of dramatic analysis. Indeed, I have borrowed the term "analytical space" from Foucault in these Williams chapters to describe this traditional notion of dramatic spatial/temporal logic, which works through a strategy of breaking off parts to construct a whole so that part and whole are mutually reinforced and reason is reinstated.

What then are Williams's ties to realism? First, the usual ones: the history and tradition of mimesis, metaphysics, and realism in the West, assumptions contained in theater construction, audience and critical response, promotion, and so on. As I have tried to show in my chapters on Williams, he is aware of the mimetic bias in the theater. More radical perhaps is the importance I place on the fact that, like O'Neill, Williams refers to specific social and political moments in his plays and places them in specific local situations—that The Glass Menagerie, for instance, anticipates, in the midst of a "memory play" time warp, the beginnings of World War II. Such references will not seem irrelevant to anyone interested in the period or in mimesis, or indeed in Williams, whose work is very relativistic, and consequently concerned with the relevance of time and place. And here the lie is given, I think, to the notion that period concerns and mimetic theory could be mutually exclusive.

In the chapter on Iceman, for example, the discussion of the divided self in its delusion of historical mastery is explored via Paul de Man's rhetoric of romanticism. But I could also point to the historical timeliness of Jacques Lacan's 1949 lecture "The Mirror Stage," in which he criticizes the existentialist notion of the self-sufficient subject. Lacan suggests that, by ignoring the fundamental division and misprision in the process of subjectivation, existentialist philosophy was a prelude to the concentration camp and its postwar urban effects. And is it necessary to add that Lacan had publicly elaborated this theory as early as 1936? (See Jacques Lacan, *Ecrits*.) Similarly, in the chapter on *A Streetcar Named Desire*, I build a case for Williams's sense of the spatial/temporal as definition, confinement, a metaphor for social control as it becomes fearfully literalized, in the tenement in *The Glass Menagerie*, or in Foucault's asylum.

There is no claim made here for either O'Neill or Williams as social realists, let alone socialist realists.[28] On the contrary, as I have argued, their direct concern with mimesis is with its assumption of a particular relation of art to life, an assumption—and a binary— each writer explicitly invokes to destroy. Williams and O'Neill recall social realism and classic realist drama "to their own motifs," as Derrida says of Artaud's strategy, in an effort, precisely, to "reawaken this tradition," to make its presence fully felt, "no longer experienced within metaphysical naiveté" (*Writing and Difference* 194).[29]

Consequently, in our current terms, "realism" and "idealism" are not poles apart. Once appearances have become, as they are in Aristotelian mimetic theory, not concealment of the truth but the very conditions in which truth can be observed, emotion and reason are no longer clearly distinguishable as motives for action. Finding the truth is not a matter, then, of intellectually rising above drama to inquiry (cf. Nussbaum 131). And when appearances include not just physical things but thoughts, and shared opinions, the very process of reasoning becomes a part of representation—which is, as his self-conscious writerliness suggests (and as Martha Nussbaum has argued [130]), exactly Plato's object in writing his dialogues. As a result of this murkiness of the "real" and the "ideal," I make no apology for "realism" and "mimesis" as vexatious terms in what follows, which is intended neither as a defense of realism nor as an attempt to humble it before some new and higher truth. Indeed, as I have tried to show, realist drama, which takes the representation of appearances to hitherto undreamed-of lengths and depths, provides me with the conditions for these perceptions.

2 Long Day's Journey into Night
The Seen and the Unseen

> What is tragic is not the impossibility but the necessity
> of repetition.
>
> —Jacques Derrida

The characters in Long Day's Journey into Night find themselves creating a new kind of religion, in which they experience, not sin without guilt, but guilt without sin—the habit of belief without its antecedent. In the circular strategy of the play, the characters revise their pasts to fit their own truths. And in this revision lies an impossible search for origins. (Who did what? When?) Without a cause, a center, the meaning of their suffering keeps eluding them. The endless discussions burrow deeper and deeper after that elusive first cause, pushing up layers of truth, revealing the strata of personal strategies that relativize it beyond recognition. If it were possible to say that something could be more lost, Long Day's Journey into Night could be described as a play in which what is lost in the beginning becomes progressively, hopelessly, implacably lost. The apparent illogic of this description, which seems to roll up the logic of representation, nevertheless echoes the play itself. In act 2, Tyrone says to Mary, "If you're that far gone in the past already, when it's only the beginning of the afternoon, what will you be tonight?" (86). Mary, as the line suggests, represents a challenge to representation: the idea that a character has the power at once to be and not to be.

"Being" seems to demand a referent, just as language demands an auditor—becomes "dialogue." Realistic drama provides a motivation for dialogue, a reason for being. It promises a fullness of meaning, a logic that connects character and action through a mediating language. Language, and the reality it purports to convey, are representable as communication: the motivated self-revelation of one character to another. Thoughts are *connected* through dialogue; they become lucid and perceptible. Similarly, the material world is subsumed into consciousness, as the object of that consciousness. In the language of realism, mimesis attains its formal perfection in a tautological assumption: that the truth is representable and that what is representable is truth. In *Long Day's Journey* the lines of connection are tenuous: language doesn't seem to connect truth with experience, or to connect character with character, or to connect character with the material world. As the play wears on, the characters seem less "motivated," the "dialogue" more diffuse, and material reality more dense, opaque, threatening, an obstacle course by act 4. "What will you be tonight?" Tyrone's question to Mary is a rhetorical one, and the play does not answer it.

"[W]ho ever said the theater was created to analyze a character, to resolve the conflicts of love and duty . . . ?" Artaud asks (41). In the drama of realism, the revelation of character through dialogue is of the first importance. For Aristotle, plot is the first essential for tragedy, character the second (*On the Art of Poetry* 40). But in modern "bourgeois" theater, as Lukács describes it, character "becomes everything," "since the conflict is entirely for the sake of character's vital centre; . . . because the force disposed of by this vital centre alone determines the dialectic, that is, the dramatic, quality of drama" (Bentley 435). Brecht put this another way, speaking of dramatic (as opposed to epic) theater: "thought determines being" (37). Aristotle says that thought "comes out in what [the characters] say when they are proving a point or expressing an opinion" (*On the Art of Poetry* 39); it is, in other words, the meaning in the dialogue.

In dramatic (mimetic) theater, then, dialogue "determines" character; and as Lukács says, character is the ground that determines "dialectic," the dramatic or dialogic (logic-of-dialogue), in drama. Dialogue and character depend on each other, and as character gains in importance on the modern stage, dialogue becomes more and more heavily freighted. At the same time, the not-human world, the world of material objects, gets squeezed out by this dialogic form. The drama of Renaissance self-mirroring and after has been exclusively a drama of "interpersonal relationships" as Peter Szondi describes it in *Theory of the Modern Drama*:

> By deciding to disclose himself to his contemporary world, man transformed his internal being into a palpable and dramatic presence. The surrounding world, on the other hand, was drawn into a rapport with him because of his disclosure and thereby first achieved dramatic realization. Everything prior to or after this act was, had to remain, foreign to the drama—the inexpressible as well as the expressed, what was hidden in the soul as well as the idea already alienated from its subject. Most radical of all was the exclusion of that which could not express itself—the world of objects—unless it entered the realm of interpersonal relationships. [7]

Sich entschliessen, the reflexive verb here translated as "to disclose oneself," also means "to decide" (Szondi 118 n.7x). The "self-disclosure" of dialogue is thus, for Szondi as well as for Lukács and Brecht, self-*determining*. Character in mimetic drama is understood, circumscribed, and limited by dialogue, by dialectic. By implication, that which cannot be represented in dialogue is outside the drama, for drama *is* dialogue: "The Drama is possible only when dialogue is possible" (Szondi 10).

The relationship between character and dialogue is thus reciprocal in mimetic drama and serves two major functions: to disclose character (to describe, define, and limit it) and to determine those elements of the material world that will contribute to the character's self-expression. Character is an omnivorous life force, or "vital centre," that gathers the objective world to itself. Realistic mise-en-scène is not expressive of anything outside the dialogue; it is only meaningful as it accrues meaning via character, establishing a mimetic reciprocity between the text and the stage image. For example, in *Long Day's Journey into Night*, Mary Tyrone is associated with the windows, to which she retreats from the unpleasantness of facing the family, the light, the definiteness of objects. Realism tries to make mise-en-scène useful as a setting that identifies character and limits the scope of its action; in naturalism it is also the character-determining environment or, eventually, the expressionistic, symbolic projection of consciousness. O'Neill uses all of these scenic functions in Long Day's Journey into Night; as versions of realism, they are not incompatible. But in his play there is a curious retrograde motion in the process of self-disclosure that corresponds, interestingly enough, to the gradual assumption by the characters of the quality and status of objects, mechanical automatons.

It is, at the end of the play, as if the characters themselves had been subsumed by the mise-en-scène, instead of the other way around. By act 4, material objects seem to be obstacles to the characters' self-expression. Edmund and Jamie are each heard entering the house, bumping into things, complaining about the darkness, which, with the fog, blurs outlines and effaces boundaries between people and things. Jamie clownishly announces his own entrance after stumbling into the house and accuses the front steps of low cunning: "The fron [sic] steps tried to trample me. Took advantage of fog to waylay me. Ought to be a lighthouse out there" (155).[1] Similarly, when Edmund bumps his knee in the dark hallway, it is like the ironic success of an experiment in epistemology: offstage, outside the dialogue, things apparently exist. Not only do they exist exclusive of the character's speech and of the stage image: Jamie jokes that things have their own consciousness and take their revenge on him. Things take control when the characters no longer see them; the notion that things exist only to express the characters' ideas about themselves splits them from the objective world, making them vulnerable to it.

In fact the deep identity between character and mise-en-scène, through dialogue, is a part of realism's obeisance to the concept of human mastery of the material world through language and of the material world as an inert mass waiting for the agency of human consciousness to mold, shape, and change it. Even when environment supposedly *determines* character, in naturalism, the "objective" world's subjective importance is, if anything, only heightened. For this is only the *reverse* of the mastery narrative that lies behind realism, and ultimately its scientific assumptions create a new notion of mastery on the idea of environmental change: if environment determines character, it follows that a more desirable environment will result in a happier, more successful human being; or else the natural forces of the environment will weed out the undesirable, leaving a stronger, better adapted race that can make the most of its opportunities. In realism, then, even at its most scientifically ruthless, nothing is unalterable or insurmountable except the fact of ultimate human triumph over things.

The narrative of progressive mastery over material means and ends is also the narrative of nineteenth-century capitalist and Marxist economy. *Long Day's Journey into Night* actually opens with a story about capitalists that seldom gets more than a mention in criticism of the play.[2] In the Shaughnessy story, over which Jamie and Edmund are laughing as they enter in act 1, a lazy, good-for-nothing Irish peasant gets the better of his neighbor, a rich American capitalist, after the peasant's pigs have taken a wallow in the capitalist's ice pond. Edmund, who tells the story, is clearly on the side of the Irishman, as against the oilman, the "ruling plutocrat," while his father, hiding his Irish patriotism, calls Edmund a "socialist anarchist." Besides its introduction to an ongoing antagonism in the play between father and son, critics have pointed out that the Shaughnessy story provides the act with levity and contrast. But seen apart from these realistic functions of disclosure and coherence, it may seem, on the contrary, a very odd and significant story, especially placed in such a prominent position. It seems to call attention precisely to those stories upon which realism relies for its organization of character and material reality. The image of pigs wallowing in an ice pond is the image of a tale gone amok. And it seems to arrive in answer to Tyrone's invocation a moment before of a philosophy of objectivity and mastery: "Forget everything and face nothing! It's a convenient philosophy if you've no ambition in life" (21).

The realistic function of the story thus conveniently obscures its apparent questioning of the realistic philosophy, in which reality is "faced" and overcome, not eluded, much less denied. Shaughnessy, as it happens, wins his battle with the oil millionaire by translating the "facts" into a new narrative with himself as its hero and its victim. His manipulation of the obvious "truth" is a resourceful avoidance of conflict, as the question of how the pigs got into the pond in the first place is forgotten. Shaughnessy's story parodies the realistic association of truth with mastery and questions the validity of any narrative that asserts it. In revealing narrative as a tool for mastery, not an avenue of self-disclosure, it prefigures the strategy of the rest of the play. The complications ensuing for realistic character are untenable, cannot be "occupied." Shaughnessy, the tenant who doesn't know his place, impinges on his neighbor's territory, subverting the code of mastery and avoiding the dialogic that would reassert it: "He told me he never gave Harker a chance to open his mouth" (24).[3]

"Truth" is translatable, revisable, losing its adherence to a shared meaning. Partly the play presents this as a problem of subjectivity: "truth" frequently stands in opposition to what the characters "feel" or "believe" or how they perceive things. ("It's not true the way you look at it!" [144].) But the character that seems to be "revealed" by these subjective statements is often clouded by its objective treatment of truth as something to be molded to a strategic purpose, not expressed but mastered. A story is told, for example, that Mary tried to commit suicide by throwing herself into the ocean in the middle of the night. Tyrone reminds her of this in act 2, scene 2, where she replies by cutting off the tale, then denying it (86–87). But the story is repeated in act 3 by Mary herself, who is now trying to defend Edmund from the doctor's diagnosis of consumption. The facts of the case, she implies, are the doctor's narrative "invent[ion]," the "diagnosis" just another story. By act 3 Mary is ready to brutalize Edmund—and herself—with the same facts she had earlier denied: "You remember that, don't you?" she asks him (118).

The suicide attempt, which Tyrone "must have dreamed" in the earlier scene, turns to fact in order to prove the doctor's diagnosis a fiction. In the context of power relations, fact and fiction keep threatening to turn into each other here, like Prince Hal trying on the sleeping Henry's crown. Within the framework of recognizable conventions of realistic self-disclosure, Long Day's Journey into Night undermines the realistic notion of character: its revelation through dialogue and its verification via the mise-en-scène.

What of a character that cannot meet these conditions of representation? Does it become invisible? In Strange Interlude, O'Neill explored the possibility of revealing character through the clash of uttered and unuttered speech; that is, he tried to separate "thought" from "dialogue," with "character" falling somewhere in between. Of course, "thought" was still representable, and "dialogue" still carried the action. Interpersonal relationships still developed on the basis of what the characters said "aloud," for example, when Nina persuaded Ned to give her a baby and when Sam's mother persuaded Nina to get an abortion. But O'Neill had already opened the door to an examination of dialogue as a form that very much "determines character." The interior monologues of *Strange Interlude* might be read as O'Neill's (necessarily unsuccessful) move to expose language as a cultural product that reproduces its own meaning in narrative. "How we poor monkeys hide from ourselves behind the sounds called words!" Nina says.[4] But O'Neill cannot dodge this problem, as is evident from the many silent ellipses in the play that connect the characters' unspoken thoughts.

In *Long Day's Journey into Night*, Mary Tyrone, too, accuses herself of trying to hide behind words. Alone onstage in act 3, like Nina with her "private" thoughts, Mary is apparently free of dialogical constraints. She recites a prayer, then catches herself: "You expect the Blessed Virgin to be fooled by a lying dope fiend reciting words! You can't hide from her!" (107). Mary's attempt to repent, to save herself, here is, interestingly, an attempt at dialogue: she is, after all, speaking to someone. But she catches herself "lying" and "reciting words," relying on the Virgin's presence, just as she has relied on Cathleen's presence for her earlier speeches in act 3. In the form of the dialogic, Mary seeks to define herself, even to redeem herself. She cuts off her dialogue in the recognition of its false "determination" of character, its masklike quality as something she "hides" behind. Unlike the other Tyrones, Mary is neither actor nor poet by profession, and she finds the mask constraining. Earlier in the act she tells Cathleen: "I've never had the slightest desire to be an actress," and "I've never felt at home in the theater" (102). But the role she (naively) rejects is uttered in a metatheatrical moment that reveals, if anything, the difficulty of her own representation. Mary becomes more and more in the play the symbol of a loss not easy to represent, and her lines betray the knowledge of this transformation. After act 3 she is no longer even on the stage until the play's final moments.

Actors, poets, and addicts are character types that manage to obviate the need for "motivation": they are presented as experts at dissimulation. Their attention, in other words, is always deflected a bit away from the scene, so as to steal—and reveal—it. These characters set up circumstances in which character fails to remain stable, in which language fails to reveal a wholeness of meaning. At this point "realism" is exposed by its own technique. *Long Day's Journey into Night* is about a family of self-conscious performers who have never been without the audience of the other Tyrones. More completely than *Strange Interlude*, with its ménage à quatre, this later play interrogates the impossibility of the ego's self-presence, the constant muddying of motivation and desire by the presence of another. For, like God, the family always precedes the self.

As the men desert the house at the end of act 3, Mary keeps reminding them that they are "acting": "You're so like your father, dear," she tells Edmund. "You love to make a scene out of nothing so you can be dramatic and tragic" (120). When Tyrone insists that Edmund won't die, Mary says, "You don't believe that! I can tell when you're acting!" (122). Ironically, much of the playacting in *Long Day's Journey* is occasioned by Mary, by the need to protect her and to isolate her. But as she isn't fooled by these acts, and as she withdraws from the play, the question is, whom is this acting meant to deceive? Mary feels entrapped by the falseness of the men, spied upon; theirs is a cruel kindness. Already by the end of act 2, she expresses ambivalence about the presence of the other characters, even in her loneliness: "It's so lonely here. (Then her face hardens into bitter self-contempt.) You're lying to yourself again. You wanted to get rid of them. Their contempt and disgust aren't pleasant company. You're glad they're gone. (She gives a little despairing laugh.) Then Mother of God, why do I feel so lonely?" (95). The circularity of this speech encloses a myth of self-reliance ("You're glad they're gone") that cannot help returning to its "loneliness," its rhetorical gesture toward dialogue. Unable to be alone without her drama of loneliness, Mary moves one step away from the dialogic she will have abandoned altogether by her disappearance in act 4.

Yet her presence remains a constant for the other characters, who "act" for her even when she isn't there. In act 4 Mary's symbolic function as the representation of loss is the only explicit motivation sustaining the dialogue. Mary, like Nina Leeds, becomes a space or battleground across and around which dialogue remains possible— even necessary.[5] Her presence gives the other characters their raison d'être—or at least their reason to "act," to "be dramatic." Nina

Leeds, Mary's forerunner, sees herself very much as this symbolic space: "My three men! . . . I feel their desires converge in me! . . . to form one complete beautiful male desire which I absorb . . . and am whole. . . . they dissolve in me, their life is my life" (*Complete Plays* 756).[6] Nina, as the convergence of male desires, represents a locus of plot, of narrative; and this position, like Mary's, excludes her from the language of disclosure and self-representation.

Teresa de Lauretis has argued that, in modern theories of subjectivity (specifically, semiotics and psychoanalysis), woman does not *cohere* in language, precisely because she occupies that *space* which makes representation possible: "[T]he position of woman in language . . . is one of non-coherence; she finds herself only in a void of meaning, the empty space between the signs . . . a place not represented, not symbolized, and thus preempted to subject (or self) representation" (8). Similarly, the woman in O'Neill's plays seems to exceed the limits of character, to be a kind of goal for what de Lauretis describes as the Oedipal narrative of quest and conquest, the place of narrative origin and connection. Nina is explicitly a womb in which narrative ("desire") converges and forms. Mary, as the religious significance of her name implies, is more ethereal a presence, a spirit hovering and brooding over the male characters, perpetuating their dialogue long after she has left the stage. As de Lauretis suggests, the woman constitutes a challenge to representation, a negativity propping up the signs and distinguishing them from one another, speaking in their silent spaces.

Mary's negativity is made representable by her morphine addiction, which increasingly cuts her off from the men and from the dialogue. Her distance from them is manifested, in fact, by her inability to carry on dialogue, at which the men abandon her to her loneliness, with the excuse that *she* has abandoned *them*: "It's you who are leaving us, Mary" (83). Artaud's emphasis on materialization, on mise-en-scène, expresses the desire for a theater that need not depend on language. "The theater itself," he writes, " . . . lives only by materialization" (108). If in realistic drama dialogue is revelation, in Artaudian theater it only obscures meaning:

> All true feeling is in reality untranslatable. To express it is to betray it. But to translate it is *to dissimulate it*. True expression hides

insists that people *cannot* change. Morphine may, as its name punningly suggests, have transformational qualities, but in this play it becomes symbolic of *irreversible* transformation—of, perhaps, change itself, the one thing that never changes. A careful reading of *Long Day's Journey into Night* reveals that the characters insist, over and over again, from the beginning of the play, that change is impossible. Most of these references are either given to Mary or made about her, and by the end of the play it is clear that she represents to all the characters a kind of fatality. If Mary is a "ghost" by act 4, Jamie, Tyrone, and Edmund have been similarly drained of their agency as characters: they play cards "mechanically," succumb to oblivion through whiskey, and seem, in the final stage direction, unable even to move. This close affinity between transformation and the denial of change is suggested through Mary's associations with morphine and fog. She first moves to "the windows at right" on the line, "Thank heavens, the fog is gone" (17). Mary is the first to call attention to this metaphor, and it remains a barometric indicator of her growing need to escape, and later, of her surrender to this need. Already by act 2, scene 2 the metaphor is a shorthand between Tyrone and Mary through which they escape confrontation:

> TYRONE: (Trying to speak naturally) Yes, I spoke too soon.
> We're in for another night of fog, I'm afraid.
> MARY: Oh, well, I won't mind it tonight.
> TYRONE: No, I don't imagine you will, Mary.
> MARY: (Flashes a glance at him. . . .)
> [82]

But the fog, which enters the dialogue through Mary and becomes itself the language for her illness, is of course associated with all the characters and even with the play itself. The fog, Mary says, makes one feel "that everything has changed, and nothing is what it seemed to be" (98). Edmund, like Mary, responds to this transforming power; when he was out in the fog, he tells Tyrone, "Nothing was what it is" (131). These complicated statements, where the fog has a morphine effect of permanent change, both assert and deny referential meaning, subordinating realistic objective logic to a new logic of perception. "Don't look at me as if I'd gone nutty," Edmund says. "I'm talking sense. Who wants to see life as it is, if they can help it?" (131). But the language Edmund uses to describe his perceptions is still the language of "faithful realism" (154). While he aspires to "poetry" he falls short, and "realism" is the result, faute de mieux, an inadequate, even inarticulate language Edmund calls "stammering": "Stammering is the native eloquence of us fog people" (154).

Critics who have felt comfortable interpreting this line as an auto-biographical reference to O'Neill's own sense of inadequacy as a writer, and so to his return, thus late in his life, to "realistic" form, risk missing the line's criticism of realism, and its claim to "native eloquence." "Fog people" are "drowned," dead; Edmund describes feeling like "a ghost within a ghost," "walking on the bottom of the sea" (131). Fog and sea merge, for Edmund, in a liquid that en-velops and dissolves him, and from this union comes a language both stammering *and* eloquent, inadequate yet "faithful," somehow "native," expressive of his "home." Edmund's "realism" is a lan-guage of stuttering imperfection, stumbling over the obvious like an obstacle in the dark. In a similarly contradictory language, the sound of the foghorn in the play is almost always accompanied by the sound of ships' bells, and so each reminder is also a warning, in a kind of endless movement between the past and future, an antici-pation outside of time. These alarms bother Mary less once she is transformed by morphine, but they signal a danger in the amor-phousness of self-immersion: it isn't complete until the self is lost forever.[8] The foghorn, like Tyrone's snoring, wakes the old distinc-tions, "keeps reminding you, and warning you, and calling you back" (99), interrupting the pull toward stasis, the merging that looks a lot like death.

Talk is useless: this point too the play makes repeatedly (44–45, 75, 78, 93, 132, 173), from its first pages, when Mary and Tyrone simulate a "dialogue" that circles politely around concern, resent-ment, defensiveness, and denial: "We'll have no talk of reducing" (14); "I know it's a waste of breath trying to convince you" (15). Within as well as between the characters, conflict surfaces, is inter-rupted, and resubmerges without resolution.

MARY: Oh, James, please! You don't understand! I'm so worried about Edmund! I'm so afraid he—

TYRONE: I don't want to listen to your excuses, Mary.

MARY: (Strickenly.) Excuses? You mean—? Oh, you can't believe that of me! You mustn't believe that, James! (Then slip-
ping away into her strange detachment—quite casually.)
Shall we not go into lunch, dear? I don't want anything but I
know you're hungry.
(He walks slowly to where she stands in the doorway. He
walks like an old man. As he reaches her she bursts out
piteously.)
James! I tried so hard! I tried so hard! Please believe—!

TYRONE: (Moved in spite of himself—helplessly.) I suppose
you did, Mary.
(Then grief-strickenly.)
For the love of God, why couldn't you have the strength to
keep on?

MARY: (Her face setting into that stubborn denial again.)
I don't know what you're talking about. Have the strength to
keep on what?

TYRONE: (Hopelessly.) Never mind. It's no use now. [69–70]

Act 2, scene 1 ends with this scene between Tyrone and Mary, in
which the double dynamic of internal/external revision denies conflict and resolution. Like Shaughnessy and Harker, they never engage;
they avoid the scene. The strategy of avoidance is employed by the
other characters as well; it is a hallmark of O'Neill's dramatic writing, a technique by which he seeks to express a layered, unstable
consciousness that renders dialogic formulas impotent. At the same
time, dialogue must go on, and its reaffirmation is achieved at the
cost of a whole "truth": something must be denied for the play
to be representable.[9] In Long Day's Journey, the characters long to forget,
but "[t]hat's what makes it so hard—for all of us," Mary tells
Edmund. "We can't forget" (48). The submerged complications of
truth keep resurfacing in the dialogue, causing moments of extraordinary self-conscious revisionism. When Mary's memories reveal to
Edmund new reasons for her persistent illness, reasons that suggest
Tyrone as a cause, Tyrone says, "Mary! Can't you forget—?" And
Mary answers, "No, dear. . . . I'm sorry I remembered out loud"
(113–14). In act 1, Tyrone accuses Jamie of mocking everyone but

himself. "JAMIE: (Wryly) That's not true, Papa. You can't hear me talking to myself, that's all. TYRONE: (Stares at him puzzledly, then quotes mechanically) 'Ingratitude, the vilest weed that grows'!" (32).

The dialogue lurches on, beyond these appearances of another life it is not disclosing, as if it were a mechanical windup toy, as if the characters were part of its mechanism. The result is not a sense of reality behind a mask, however; on the contrary, what is "revealed" by the slips and interruptions in the dialogue is the actor behind the character. Logically the consequence is an ever-increasing loss of security and authenticity in the character and a growing sense of the reality of the mask. Act 4, in which Mary is absent and the men get down to it—to "understanding" and "in vino veritas stuff," is a complex masterpiece of theatrical quotation, posturing, and self-deferral.

The sudden rush of poetry in act 4 is not transcendent, revelatory of some unifying principle, but intertextual, shattering, ironic. Like the fragments in Eliot's *Waste Land*, which the act seems in many ways to echo, the quotations create a tissue of mutually parodic commentaries. They explode out of the scene, making mock connections between the imaginary present in the theater and its literary tradition, tearing the face from the character and the act, replacing them with their verso, as Artaud would say, their mocking face. Tyrone is right to take Jamie's and Edmund's poetry as a challenge to him, a weapon in their combat, for Baudelaire, Wilde, and Swinburne are revisions of his Bardolatry, just as surely as Jamie's "trained seals" are a swipe at Edwin Booth.

> TYRONE: Why can't you remember your Shakespeare and forget the third-raters. You'll find what you're trying to say in him—as you'll find everything else worth saying. (He quotes, using his fine voice.) "We are such stuff as dreams are made on, and our little life is rounded with a sleep."
> EDMUND: (Ironically) Fine! That's beautiful. But I wasn't trying to say that. We are such stuff as manure is made on, so let's drink up and forget it. That's more my idea. [131]

The rhythm of reversal and revision that typifies this act is a specifically modernist revisionism, of ironic quotation, juxtaposition, and fragmentation. It is thus aimed at undermining the old order, and indeed Jamie and Edmund use it to pull God, Shakespeare, Mammon, and Edwin Booth out from under Tyrone like so many rugs. It is striking that in the act of *Long Day's Journey* that claims the most truth, honesty, and understanding, O'Neill fractures the imaginary world of secure values and replaces it with quotation, with that which undermines language's originality and authenticity. By constantly referring to other texts, he denies the play any sense of its own self-disclosure, "placing" it, to use the modernist term, making it a stage for literary self-dramatization. Quotation becomes, in act 4, like Tyrone's "mechanical" quotation in act 1, a reflex of the dialogue, a self-reflexive act of the literary text, not a reflection of "character"'s unique identity. Instead of creating a dialogue between characters, it creates a dialogue between texts, in which "character" functions as a textual crossing.

There is a back-and-forth switching of actor-audience roles among the characters here as well, which begins with Tyrone turning on the lightbulbs of the chandelier. "That's a grand curtain," Edmund says approvingly. "(He laughs.) You're a wonder, Papa" (128). At the end of the act, Jamie provides Mary's entrance with a stage direction. "The Mad Scene. Enter Ophelia!" Edmund fiercely slaps his mouth. "Good boy, Edmund. The dirty blackguard! His own mother!" Tyrone says, supplying both applause and moral commentary (170). In their praise of each other's performance, the men keep underlining the improvisational quality of character, as if they are trying on effects for each other. It's no wonder, then, that Edmund's "understanding" of Tyrone is enhanced by the Edwin Booth story, in which one actor's praise for another results in a new character: old "Gaspard," the miser. At the end of the speech, Tyrone is thoroughly in the grip of his own theater: "(He glances vaguely at his cards.) My play, isn't it?" And immediately after, he clicks out the lightbulbs, one by one, to the accompaniment of a kind of reprise—and Edmund's "ironical laughter" (150–51).

But the irony is deeper here than the mere contradiction between Tyrone's words and his action. It lies in the way he, to use Derrida's definition of "repetition," defers himself in order to maintain himself (*Writing and Difference* 245). He mourns the loss of the little piece of paper on which he had recorded Booth's praise of his Othello. "Where is it now, I wonder? Somewhere in this house. I remember

I put it away carefully—EDMUND: (With a wry ironical sadness.) It might be in an old trunk in the attic, along with Mama's wedding dress" (152). Picking up Tyrone's similarity to Mary, and her deferral to a "lost" "true self," Edmund's lines show the irony and the tragedy in the reading that is always rereading, the "for a time" that has always yet to be (150, 176). Then, as if aware that once again the dialogic impulse has been threatened, he "adds quickly," "For Pete's sake, if we're going to play cards, let's play" (152).

The need to perpetuate dialogue, as if something could be exchanged, or revealed, or translated by it, drives the notion of "character" out into the open. "The conflict," as Lukács says of modern drama, "is entirely for the sake of character's vital centre" (Bentley 435). Character needs dialogue in order to save itself. There is no longer a question about whether dialogue simply *reveals* character; the dialogic form is not an expression of the character—it never was. Character is an expression of the form. O'Neill thought this was what "tragedy" was about: our attempt to make something express us, instead of realizing that *we* are the expression (Cargill, Fagin, and Fisher 125–26).

Derrida's remark about tragedy makes O'Neill's point differently. For Derrida, what is tragic is that the drama can always and only repeat the loss of its object, the referent whose absence keeps the drama in play. The "memory" and "forgetting" so common to plays of the modern period are translations of this philosophic idea of a theater, this shade or "ghost" of a meaning that Artaudian theater reveals as a "mask." *Long Day's Journey* is a play of Artaudian "necessity" and "rigor" (cf. Derrida 238), that is, a play that plays out the tragedy of repetition. As such, its tragedy has been played before, the characters know their roles by heart, and they stay pretty much, if rebelliously at times, in character. With its careful adherence to dramatic unities, the play shows up the tragedy implicit in "metatheatre," [10] the drama's self-consciousness about its own form: it is the form of the rehearsal, or repetition, of a drama that is always just about to be played. Indeed, O'Neill had to work hard to give all those dramatic unities some sense of unity and completion. In fact as Mary announces in act 2 (87), there is no difference between the past, present, and future, and consequently no sequence, no causality, no return to an ending or origin. There is no change from one state to another nor any direction for change to take. Is it the "past" the characters can't forget? or *remember*? It seems just as true to say they don't remember the "*present*," the ostensible "action" of the play they are all ready to perform, for struggling after that "past."[11] At the same time, the perpetual audience of the other characters, the demand of the dialogic, seems to split character from itself. Character slides from the temporal distinction of past/present toward the ontological distinction of presence/absence.

Mary, who has warned her sons that one changes by imperceptible degrees, "until at last everything comes between you and what you'd like to be, and you've lost your true self forever" (61), represents this split. She becomes almost invisible, "ghostly," her language not a dialogue, spoken in a present that slips away into the past, seated by the windows, thin transparencies on the night and fog. "She'll listen but she won't listen. She'll be here but she won't be here" (78). Like the men, Mary seems gradually to be absorbed into the mise-en-scène. But unlike them she loses her solidity, becoming watery and insubstantial. As we have seen, Mary is necessary to the play's dialogic, in which she becomes increasingly symbolic, etherealized, as the barometer of value, the mother, the mother/whore, the haven and the lure. The men, whose fear of her is explicit by act 4—their fear, in fact, *motivates* the act's *inertia*, its rush of *language*—nonetheless repeatedly invoke her presence. Perhaps nowhere in realistic domestic drama has the mother been so clearly revealed as the figure of male fear and desire.

Mary represents the space of the dramatic action, its obstacle and its goal, but also the watery insubstantiality of these things, with her morphine transformations, her association with windows, night, and fog, and her relativistic relation to time and causality.[12] "The past is the present, isn't it? It's the future too" (87). In revisions, O'Neill struggled to give the play a sense of progression and closure through Mary, and Mary's line does close the play: "I fell in love with James Tyrone and was so happy for a time" (176). But by these same revisions, O'Neill increased Mary's symbolic presence, and consequently the central ambivalence and relativism of the play's structure, so that the "finality" he achieves with Mary's last line reverberates unsettlingly. "The truth is representable," that realistic doctrine, depends on our knowing that what *is* can't *not* be. With Mary Tyrone's representation of invisibility, O'Neill gives that truth the lie.[13]

3   The Iceman Cometh
Buying Time

But, bejees, something ran over me!
Must have been myself, I guess.

—*The Iceman Cometh,* act 3

For to know inauthenticity is not the same as to be authentic.

—Paul de Man

In realistic drama, there is the illusion that the present can be dramatized. This assumption is based upon an idea of "history" that rationalizes the movement of time on "natural" or biological models. Ironically, then, realism finds itself needing to emphasize *past* time. The exposition telescopes action into a present totality (i.e., inclusive of the past) that reinforces the notion of linear or cyclical history (plot). The future is by implication *not* dramatizable; it is only imaginable, and the purpose of realistic drama is objectively to imitate the present reality and not to be fanciful. On the stage, the catastrophe is resolved, the problem localized or exorcised, usually through death or some other moral expedient recognized by the middle-class spectator of the time. This comforting closure of realism, again ironically, reinforces the pastness of the action, its safe distance from the spectator, and so its illusion.[1] This is the reassuring past tense to which one is so accustomed in the realistic novel, and perhaps we could define illusion, on the basis of such illusionism, as the experience of the present seen as a safely objective past.

Thus illusion, in the realistic tradition of modern European and American theater, is based on a contradiction: that we can dramatize an objective present, and yet that this present moment is really only a recapitulation of the past, which the present determines and explains. The notion that the present can somehow be recognized consciously as the logical result of the past was of course what Shaw objected to in realism: the implication that "reality" was fixed and inevitable, or at least inevitably *clear*, like a well-made plot. With the "discussion," which he learned from Ibsen, Shaw stopped the machine of realistic plotting while characters debated each other's versions of reality. (Roughly there were two versions, or so Shaw pretended: realism and idealism.) Similarly, O'Neill, in a 1924 interview, saw that modern plays were now concerned with people's *inner* struggles and that that concern made them "plotless" (Cargill, Fagin, and Fisher 111). Theorists of drama and the novel have noted that what Tennessee Williams calls the "contemplative" state of the theater is not the state we live in; that the objective present of the drama has no necessary connection to the flux we narrativize as "history." Thus Georg Lukács, writing in 1909:

> Since the vital centre of character and the intersecting point of man and his destiny do not necessarily coincide, supplemental theory is brought in [in modern drama] to contrive a dramatic linkage of the two. One could indeed say that the maintenance of personality is threatened by the totality of external data. The data perhaps cannot drain the personality dry—but personality can, by a process of internalization, seek to flee the individual data, avoiding them, keeping out of contact with them.
> [Bentley 436–37]

Character, the central concern of modern drama for Lukács, is not necessarily arrived at or explained by "external data." Indeed, there is no reason to suppose that what is crucial to character will ever enter the plot. In other words, history as dramatic narrative does not account for the self: "The data, actions manifested in the external world, fail to account for the whole man, who in turn is not able to arrive at an action revelatory of his entire self" (Bentley 436).[2]

This struggle "to arrive at an action" resembles Susanne Langer's attempt to define drama, fifty years after Lukács, as that which moves "toward something beyond," a present tension between past and future (307–308). The dramatic present is, for Langer, a poise between two states that are equally imaginative, "conceptual" structures. Her very formulation of this point echoes O'Neill's *Strange Interlude*: for Nina Leeds, as for most of O'Neill's characters, the irrevocable events of life occur outside an objective, graspable, conscious time.[3] The desire of some modern dramatic theorists to find a practical "end" for the drama in social change hypothesizes a point at which the "contemplative" time of the theater can enter the flow of historical time in which alone change could be possible.[4] As Langer argues, even this sense of time as "continuum" is an illusion, an abstraction of "natural" growth processes (312). The idea that the historic flow of time means change, and especially a change for the better, is deeply ingrained in nineteenth-century influences upon modern drama: in capitalism, Marxism, evolutionism, positivism. But its optimistic story is based on a materialist religion that art, according to some modern dramatic theorists such as Artaud, *ought to* transform.[5]

Seeing the end of art in social action means judging value by an absolute human standard—making some human standard an absolute. Moreover, such humanist theory puts its faith in the "external data," the historic gesture, which do not necessarily explain the "whole man" and which, objective and finite, can only exist in the "conceptual structures" of past and future, that is, in consciousness. Plays that prescribe social action, propaganda plays, rely on just such a fixed, definable notion of reality and of the conscious human gesture as the master of that reality. Social and moral life are thus equivalent to sciences that the intellectual in us can analyze and control. "Fiction" in this view can become "reality," and the possibility of—and responsibility for—this transformation lies squarely in the lap of humanity itself, making the human being culpable for his or her own futility. "Damn the optimists anyway!" O'Neill wrote. "They make life so darned hopeless!" (Cargill, Fagin, and Fisher 106).

In attempting to disclose the drama "behind life," as he called it, O'Neill eschews both present and future time. Consequently he, like Lukács, is more concerned with character than with history and has little faith in the possibility that dramatic time can enter historical time. At the heart of O'Neill's so-called fatalism is the deepening conviction that dream, or consciousness, while inherently more attractive than act or historical gesture—more revelatory of the inner workings of character, of suffering—is nevertheless by definition unrealizable. "Dream" in O'Neill means the parallel track that mocks at "reality" and modifies it; the two are mutually dependent. The gap between thought and act is not a difference in time but in kind. It is unbridgeable. What is needed for us to act our dreams is not courage or strength but madness and despair.

This is not, of course, something the characters of The Iceman Cometh know about. They are caught in a cultural moment, not fully able to abstract themselves. For such an abstraction they would really have to be dead, as the play's language keeps suggesting they are. The title itself is a tease on the eroticism of this possibility. Death is always to come, is always on the point of arriving. "The present" is another name for "not yet" or "already not." Yet the language of life is a language of optimism, of possibility—in short, of being—and in this way language becomes both a mercy and a trap, a trick. The Iceman Cometh is full of the language of dream, of past and future (past as future), of possible realities. But this language is threatened by the primacy of act over thought: in the realm of language there is trouble with questions of agency. The realization of meaning's immanence is dismissed contemptuously as "dream" and "illusion." Without act, dream is foolishness, childishness. The necessary opposition between dream and act seems like an accident of time. To act will be better than to dream; to act is to be present, to be able to attribute meaning, to be in the present. And the false consolation of this imaginary fusion between thought and act is inherent in the language of "now," "yesterday," and "tomorrow." Language, unlike drama, makes time a continuum, not a belated, static thing. It is the state of possibility for action, of readiness. And so language sounds reasonable, even when it is mad—because it is hopeful: every word convinces us that we are alive and postpones our death.

Beckett's plays are of course predicated on such notions. But O'Neill does not wholly abstract time and space the way Beckett does. Confusingly, especially in a play like The Iceman Cometh, O'Neill keeps one foot in the drama of realism, in historical place and time. Like Ibsen before him and Beckett after, he dramatizes a world of people who are submerged, already dead, symbolically locked in an eternity that has thrown away the key for which they keep half-unconsciously looking.[6] Yet like Ibsen, O'Neill makes his characters part of a specific world in which they are present as objects as well as subjects. The drunks in The Iceman Cometh are contingent selves in a world of other contingent selves. The play insists that there is a life outside them, and outside the bar, and it is alien and threatening. For the characters, the world outside is no competition for their personal vision. But their language argues the other way, and brings that external life into the bar, into the dream. For this reason Hickey's salesmanship works, whether he is selling "truth" or vacuum cleaners. Even his wife becomes a fiction to him, a version of his own feelings about himself. Thus O'Neill's plays never go to the lengths of Beckett's, never create a wholly self-referential space and time and language, a closed, self-sufficient Rubik's cube of metaphysics. There remains a realistic clutter of the physical in O'Neill, even in *The Iceman Cometh*—a messy, rough-edged contingency that, like Ibsen's, makes mimesis itself seem to stand for the struggling consciousness.

The historical forces of contingency are played off in *Iceman* against the antihistorical. I have suggested the historical as language and act (as opposed to dream and inertia), though the characters do not recognize the dangers of language and of its presumed relation to action. But their language of dreaming is necessarily different from Hickey's "now" salesmanship—it is a language of the past, of repetition, an endless rehearsal of something that is not and indeed never was. If language is historical, then, the idea of history enters the play through language, because the drunks live by deferring their lives to a world elsewhere. One of the play's most persistent historical references is to "The Movement"—the anarchist revolutionary activism from which Larry, Hugo, and Parritt are all more or less on the run. "I'm through with the Movement," Larry says (10–11), but it keeps returning in the pressure of responsibility brought into the bar by Parritt, the outsider, and in language, with its innate bias toward action. Inaction and death are described in terms of movement: Jimmy is "the leader of our Tomorrow Movement" (35); "Bejees," Hope says, "I'll make your Movement move!" (54). Political action—change—in the form of "The Movement," thus takes a historical reference and a reference to historical time and turns it into a metaphor for its opposite, for what *doesn't* move.

Death and the Movement are finally united in Parritt's fall from the fire escape, but movement has meant death all along. Hickey's drummer's pitch has shown them all the fatal mistake of taking language's possibilities at their face value, of making meaning's immanence somehow *present* and thereby showing up its belatedness and its difference from gesture. Hickey forces this response because he finds the "peace" of death and closure preferable to the suspense of form.[7] But of course the opera isn't over yet: Hickey isn't dead. And until he is, death is just another metaphor, an example of the trick of language that suggests that consciousness and act lie on the same plane. Here is Hickey falling asleep near the end of act 1:

> Hell of trick to go dead on you like his. (He starts to get up but relaxes again. His eyes blink as he tries to keep them open) No, boys and girls, I've never known what real peace was until now. It's a grand feeling, like when you're sick and suffering like hell and the Doc gives you a shot in the arm, and the pain goes, and you drift off. (His eyes close) You can let yourself go at last. Let yourself sink down to the bottom of the sea. Rest in peace. There's no farther you have to go. Not a single damned hope or dream left to nag you. You'll all know what I mean after you—(He pauses—mumbles) Excuse—all in—got to grab forty winks—Drink up, everybody—on me—(The sleep of complete exhaustion overpowers him. His chin sags to his chest. They stare at him with puzzled uneasy fascination.) [85–86]

The speech about drugs and death parallels the actor's pantomime of falling asleep. The combination of speech and gesture has an eerie quality, and it fascinates the others, who are beginning to sense that death is present in the room, after all—real historical death. But in addition, Hickey's sales pitch is delivered as he himself is overcome by an insurmountable physical force. He hasn't the power to rise; his eyes close involuntarily, as if his own words were a hypnotic spell rather than a call to action and awareness. The performer's actions are in fact a reminder that "Hickey" is not in control: that is, ironically, the motivation for this inertia. The very parallel that makes his gesture appropriate to his speech undermines any causal correlation between language and gesture. Similarly, Hickey's analysis at the end of the play of his motives for killing Evelyn turn out to be an interpretation—a rationalization. His motivation lies outside the power of language to account for it. Language is incommensurate with act, yet it fills the present, the gap in action, with a language of movement, an illusion of freedom. Language follows the flow of consciousness, which is itself an action, struggling to find a connection with temporal and spatial reality. O'Neill shows that language and its object are agonizingly separated, their union in gesture a dream of autonomy and fulfillment. Like the song of Keats's nightingale, the drummer's pitch of that union is an invitation to die.

Language represents history as past and future. The present lies outside consciousness and is unimaginable. And history is revisable: fiction is the illusion of a present seen with the security of the past. This continuity and linearity of the plot, of duration, is a property of dramatic realism. There is "mimetic" time in Iceman—in the historical identification of the locale and characters; in the notion of social "types"; in the political references (all of which depend on evolutionary, linear, dialectical time) to Marxism, anarchism, capitalism; and in the play's obsession with memory. The action is in the past, and the language is of the past. Like a realistic drama, the play is in the past tense and attempts to capture a moment on the line of an objectifiably accountable history.

O'Neill works against mimetic time, however, trying to catch the points at which consciousness readjusts itself, reframing time in order to keep the ego centered and secure. The superimposition of a subjective reality onto a "realistic" or "objective" one creates a curious doubling effect, as when O'Neill deliberately chooses an autobiographical subject and scene. Such metatheater pushes the play away from illusionism and toward epic irony. Epic, says Brecht, focuses the tension on process rather than conclusion, emphasizing curves rather than linear development, what we must do rather than what we ought to do (Brecht 37). O'Neill alienates the play from persuasive language, breaking down the belief in singleness of character, interpersonal communication, action (change), emotional involvement, and the illusion of the pastness of the present. The many antirealistic techniques in Iceman—repetition, choral effect, masking, and so forth—are contrasted with a powerful mimetic evocation of specific time and place by virtue of metatheater. O'Neill's self-conscious re-creation of the lowest point in his own past gives the play an added dimension of artistic distance, so that each choice of dramatic effect seems like a statement on the belatedness of drama and of self-interpretation or memory.

O'Neill's autobiographical content here emphasizes the self-consciousness of this representation of a memory. Representation and memory seem experientially similar, and indeed realism seems to unify them. Yet what all the biographical analyses of *Iceman* painstakingly expose, again and again, is the gap between the "real" self and the "fictional" self, the self as self-representation. The play is "antirealistic" precisely because it dramatizes, through its complex use of irony, this clash between consciousness and object, between, in Lukács's terms, "self" and "external data."

O'Neill's interest in irony is profound and pervasive. Throughout his oeuvre, he tries to represent the drama of the divided self; his language looks for ways to speak the struggle of self-knowledge and self-deception, consciousness and unconsciousness, matter and spirit. Freud and Jung are brought into the struggle, as are Greek masks, expressionistic lighting and acting, and so forth. But whatever tools he uses, what matters is always the distance that separates one from oneself and so from the other. In "The Rhetoric of Temporality," Paul de Man describes the modern development of irony and allegory as rhetorical figures in criticism. Ironically, he notes, "It is a historical fact that irony becomes increasingly conscious of itself in the course of demonstrating the impossibility of our being historical" (de Man 24). In *Iceman*, rather than use interior monologues or highly self-conscious types—such as actors or writers—O'Neill creates ironic doubling and distance through a group/individual dynamic. The play's meaning relies on an objective/subjective structure: every character is a critical audience for every other character.

As the play begins, the audience attending the production is made to perceive that each character's "history" seems ironic to all the others, who are of course unable/unwilling to achieve the same distance from their own experience. Everyone is acting—self-interestedly—the role of believer, of credulous audience, for everyone else, staging the irony of metatheater. As the play opens there is nothing left to learn, for most of the characters, except their own inability to function outside the group. Hickey's technique is, appropriately, to divide and conquer. Alone, outside the perspective provided by the group mechanism, each character confronts directly that gap between consciousness and experience for which he is (uniquely) unprepared. This failure comes as no surprise to any of the others, then. It is necessarily an isolated, individual—a tragic—experience. Isolated and isolating, it confirms in the individual the ironic awareness of himself that he once felt only for the others. Now he has no part to play for anyone else; instead he becomes aware of the part he has really been playing all along, to everyone else's amusement. The shock of this revelation breaks up the group.[8]

In act 1, we seem to see the group at its lowest. Everyone is asleep, static, drunk. Everyone looks dead. Nothing happens except in language, in a fiction all the characters tacitly agree to sustain. Yet even this is a language of deadness: the jokes are tired and well known, suspense is utterly absent. And yet the characters seem contented; "I've never known more contented men," Larry says. "It isn't often that men attain the true goal of their heart's desire" (36). The play begins at a dead end. Larry's speech to Rocky tells us everything we know, and everything we need to know: "To hell with the truth! As the history of the world proves, the truth has no bearing on anything. It's irrelevant and immaterial, as the lawyers say. The lie of a pipe dream is what gives life to the whole misbegotten mad lot of us, drunk or sober. And that's enough philosophic wisdom to give you for one drink of rot-gut" (9–10).

Larry's speech sums up the play in terms of "conventional wisdom" very well. It sounds like an epitaph, not an epigraph. "Truth," if by that one means an objective truth, is "immaterial," not germane (as opposed to false), with a pun on the material basis of all historic or "realistic" truth. Here is where we found ourselves in Long Day's Journey—stuck on the problem of what to do with a truth that is not objective, that becomes more elusive the harder we strive for it, what Nina Leeds in Strange Interlude exposes as the "lie" in "life." The lie here is life; truth is death, self-annihilation. What Iceman goes on with is the double by which this metaphysical paradox is lived out and through which no peace or closure is assured. Larry's references to madness and to law turn out to be prophetic of the play's division of experience.

The irony, at this point in the play, lies in the ability of each person to view the others ironically and not himself. The split sense of self is brought out in the characters' tales. On the one hand, the self is unique and autonomous; on the other, it is part of a history, a narrative. As author of his own tale, each character provides his life with a permanent narrative intrusion,[9] an interruption of his character's "history." The duration required for the plot of his life to unfold is, in other words, interrupted by the ironic moment of commentary, the tale that has no end, that constantly repeats the gap between the real and the fictive selves, in the hopeless attempt to bridge it. It is thus in these tales that the characters seem most "real"—in the moments when we least "believe" them, in the performance within the performance. The particular poignance of these tales, however, arises not from some metatheatrical self-consciousness on the part of the characters but in their mutual "revelation" as illusion. We the audience participate knowingly in the writing of the character, and in this knowing participation we are conscious of a closeness to the drama. This is not Aristotelian catharsis but more like its opposite, epic detachment. We are now, therefore, confronted with a drama in which what is at stake is our own capacity for illusion. The power and efficacy of the imagining self are put on trial by the play, threatened with obsolescence. We are at a theater that threatens to "save" us from theater.

And suddenly, profoundly, we sense that perhaps that is what we have always been seeking in the theater without knowing it: salvation from the imagining power, the permanent systematic deferral of it. But at once we see that we love the tale more than the teller; it is always through our inventing self that we are able to respond to what is outside us. Thus our "love" and "pity," our "catharsis," is both pleasurable and purifying only because it arises from an excess: a division or doubling of character that O'Neill's drama has learned cleverly to manipulate. For Aristotle, pity and terror intensify in relation to the temporal divergence of consciousness and unconsciousness or truth and ignorance of the truth. The best way to achieve pity and terror, in fact, is when the tragic deed is interrupted by knowledge (On the Art of Poetry 50). In Brecht's revision of Aristotle, ignorance is not given so high a place. Such manipulation for "psychological" effect (57) turns the action into "a hypnotic experience" (78)—not an occasion for reasoned observation.

Brecht implies, I think, that Aristotle's manipulation requires a false totality of character, a reliance on psychological coherence, on knowledge of "the truth": "the plot leads the hero into situations where he reveals his innermost being" (87). This innermost being is "driven into the open" and "then of course comes to stand for Man with a capital M" (ibid.). Thus it is a small step, according to Brecht, from an individual psychological totality to a universal "Man" who leaves the audience little opportunity—or reason—to reflect, "so that in a performance of Oedipus one has for all practical purposes an auditorium full of little Oedipuses, an auditorium full of Emperor Joneses for a performance of The Emperor Jones" (ibid.). The difference between Aristotle and Brecht here is that for Brecht there is no "truth" waiting in the wings to surprise the character— or rather, that the truth is always theoretically available, via human reason. The space between truth and ignorance is not temporal, as it is for Aristotle, but qualitative: the distance is bridged by reason, and this journey is the subject of the play. As Brecht puts it, in "dramatic theatre" "the human being is taken granted," while in "epic theatre" s/he is "the object of the inquiry" (37). In The Iceman Cometh O'Neill makes the character observable through the fiction, by implying that the spectator constructs the fiction him or herself, in complicity with the actor.

The play takes some trouble to explore the myth of "pity," in fact, the "not-me" pity of the Aristotelian spectator who, as Brecht says, "is involved in something" instead of being made to "face" it (37). "[T]he damned pity—the wrong kind, as Hickey said!" (258). This pity is a doubling back, a tactic of self-protection and self-perpetuation. Larry has it and cannot abandon his "grandstand" spectator's position. His eyes open in "self-derision" at his own pity when he prays for Parritt, "God rest his soul in peace." When he recognizes the selfishness of this automatic "selflessness," the bad faith in which he makes this prayer, Larry can, at least for a moment, envision his own death—"Be God, I'm the only real convert to death Hickey made here"(258).

Hickey's attitude toward the others seems unsentimental, disinterested, and Larry observes that there is something "inhuman" about this. But in the end it seems that Hickey is trying, like Rocky, to sell everyone else his "peace" (222)—and this sales pressure makes him unconvincing. Hickey's apparent absence of pity relies on an optimistic faith in reason that Brecht might applaud; but it, too is a position maintained by illusion, which serves the purpose of maintaining illusion. In other words, it's the kind of pity Hickey himself inveighs against: "the kind that lets itself off easy by encouraging some poor guy to go on kidding himself with a lie" (115). He still relies on the ironic doubling of the "pipe dream"; the irony of the group dynamic returns when Hope has to corroborate Hickey's story that he's insane.

The idea that Hickey may indeed be "insane" instead of having "the game of life licked" (225) subverts the temporality of a "plot" that would have seen his arrival as a catalyst for change, a motivation, instead of just another interruption of narrative. "The Iceman Cometh." And the action is deferred through language, built into language's innate optimism, its dissimulating, doubling property. Hickey's need of language increases as his capacity for self-irony—his sense that the joke may be on him—comes dangerously close to the surface. "[I]f yuh want a confession," Rocky says to the cops, "all yuh got to do is listen. He'll be tellin' all about it soon. Yuh can't stop de bastard talkin' " (231). Hickey's reflection on his own madness, his invention of "a form of himself that is 'mad' but that does not know its own madness," his "consciousness of madness," is a supreme irony, a de Manian irony of irony (de Man 216, 218). By taking irony to its extreme he is, ironically, able to take the fall for the others. He has blocked off the return from the fictional to the historical or "empirical" self, denied the closing of the gap between them. O'Neill demonstrates the implications of this visually. In act 4 he has set the bar's chairs far apart, split the characters to the Right and Left of the stage. There is no single group and no center. The relationship of back room and front room mimics act 1.

There is thus no real progression in the play, no move into the real, the present, no stage beyond irony that leads to a synthesis of reality and idea (cf. de Man 220). But The Iceman Cometh seems to promise such a synthesis all along; we have been caught up in what looks like a "plot" developing or about to develop. O'Neill models the suspense of his form on the thriller or murder mystery, and between acts 1 and 4 he creates a growing tension, a warfare of each character against himself, each against the other, and all against Hickey. Tellingly, this tension is produced at the expense of the characters' drunkenness. As their sobriety increases, so does their angry, explosive divisiveness. But Hickey, the mastermind, the plotter, mistakenly assumes he can make the present finally arrive, the Parousia that brings peace, the indicative tense. And in the fascinating reversal of act 4, he becomes entrapped in his own plot, caught in time, just like any other character. He has not beaten the game of life, after all.

In act 2 the characters are already unable to get drunk, no matter how much they drink. Hickey's proselytizing has thrown a cold shower on their agreeable personae, making them more aggressively self-protective. Harry Hope and Jimmy Tomorrow arrive together for Harry's birthday party.

> Both have been drinking heavily. In HOPE the effect is apparent only in a bristling, touchy, pugnacious attitude. It is entirely different from the usual irascible beefing he delights in and which no one takes seriously. Now he really has a chip on his shoulder. JIMMY, on the other hand, is plainly drunk, but it has not had the desired effect, for beneath a pathetic assumption of gentlemanly poise, he is obviously frightened and shrinking back within himself. [136]

Despite their lack of faith in their conventions of dissimulation,[10] the characters try to act their parts anyway. The act no longer fools even themselves. At Hickey's prompting, Harry tries to cancel out his defensive ugliness toward the others.

> HOPE (Looking guilty and shamefaced now—forcing an unconvincing attempt at his natural tone) Bejees, they ain't as dumb as you. They know I was only kidding them. They know I appreciate their congratulations. Don't you, fellers? (There is a listless chorus of "Sure, Harry," "Yes," "Of course we do," etc. He comes forward to the two girls, with JIMMY and HICKEY following him, and pats them clumsily) Bejees, I like you broads. You know I was only kidding. (Instantly they forgive him and smile affectionately.) [137]

Hope's lame apology, and the "instant" forgiveness it gets him, show how O'Neill makes us care more about the characters the less we believe what they're saying. Like an audience, the characters create each other, and in their unconvincing performances they seem piercingly real, closer to the audience than when they "believed" in their own reality. The power of the play increases as the characters are drained of all character.

They become less themselves the more Hickey tries to move them from "dream play" to "realism," from ironic distance to the ostensible "now" of an historic moment. "Yes," he tells Jimmy Tomorrow, "it's today at last" (138). "[Y]ou don't want to let yourself duck out of it by being too drunk to move—not this time!" (139). Hickey wants "tomorrow" to fuse with "today" in the moment of a historic gesture. His "present" to Harry Hope is a watch engraved with the date; his plan for them all is to force them suddenly into a reality, a present, in which, for the moment, Hickey thinks he himself is living: "You'll be in a today where there is no yesterday or tomorrow to worry you. . . . This peace is real! It's a fact! I know! Because I've got it! Here! Now! Right in front of you!" (147–48). Hickey offers himself as the incarnation, the Real Presence. And he gives the others a little crumb of the truth when he tells them that Evelyn is not in the hay with the iceman, as they have supposed, but dead and "at peace." He gives them, in short, just enough truth to make them believe in him a little, and this keeps him in the game, believing in himself a little longer.

By act 3 the characters are clinging desperately to their desire to act out their usual roles as they ascend relentlessly into sobriety. But the ascent is paralleled by a descent in the level of their humanness. As they come less and less to believe in the conventions that made them a group, they retreat more and more into the aggressive, self-defensive posture of animals. Hickey succeeds, in this act, at getting some of the characters to perform the historic gesture that is supposed to make them real. But it is a Pyrrhic victory. The merging of self and history, the loss of irony, is perceived as a descent, as a fall, and as the death of a self that has folded back on itself, recto and verso.

In act 2 there has already been a brief "scuffle" between Lewis and Wetjoen, at which Rocky is "astonished" and "amused" (130). But in act 3 the violence intensifies. You've got to kill your pipe dreams, Hickey tells them, "like I did mine" (189). And indeed the threat of leaving the bar, leaving the comfort of the divided self, brings out an eruption (a break) of murderous violence. Like a mirror of subconscious violence (the real content of Hickey's message), the set, in this act, gives prominence, for the only time in the play, to the "front room," and we see less of the "back room" than in any other act. The little united nations breaks up, without its group/individual dynamic, into powerful animal tension: Rocky and Chuck fight, then team up in a racial attack on Joe, using guns and knives (167–68); Lewis and Wetjoen "start the Boer war" again. Everyone fights in this act: Mosher fights McGloin, Jimmy Tomorrow throws his drink at Hickey. Rocky's language about his "stable" and Hugo's slips about iced champagne and enslaving the proletariat get uglier and more ominous. The dialogue between Larry and Parritt early in the act culminates in Larry's implicit suggestion that Parritt commit suicide.

> LARRY: And how about you? Be God, if you had any guts or decency—! (he stops guiltily.)
> PARRITT: (Sneeringly) I'd take that hop off your fire escape you're too yellow to take, I suppose? [162]

By the end of the act, the mood has darkened until Hugo feels he's dying (201), Harry Hope feels "like a corpse" (200), and even Hickey loses his temper for the first time (203). Hickey's game of divide and conquer, of forcing each person to be alone with himself, without an ironic "double," has resulted in degeneration, devolution. As their privileged, protected sense of self collapses, their language gets meaner, their actions become "lifeless, automatic" (206). Harry Hope calls his idolized wife a "nagging bitch" and then complains that the whiskey has no kick: "I want to pass out like Hugo. . . . Let's all pass out. Who the hell cares?" (202, 203). Things are not winding down in this act but breaking down, and Hickey seems to be losing control, losing his confidence in the peace he wants to sell.

Not only is the brute beneath the social animal that Hickey's plan reveals ugly without his illusions, but he is also motionless, purposeless, and even less free. "Bejees," Hope says before his trial with the automobile, "you bums want to keep me locked up in here's if I was in jail! I've stood it long enough! I'm free, white and twenty-one, and I'll do as I damned please, bejees!" (193). Hope of course thinks his lack of options is the fault of the others, but throughout the act the warnings have been otherwise. When an action does erupt out of the tension, it results in stalemate, in the frustration of action.

Hickey's presence is like a mirror that makes the others suddenly self-conscious, embarrassed, as if they had reached up and found an ass's head. "That's it! Murder each other, you damned loons, with Hickey's blessing!" Larry says as Joe "springs from behind the lunch counter with the bread knife in his hand" (168). "Didn't I tell you he'd brought death with him? (His interruption startles them. They pause to stare at him, their fighting fury suddenly dies out and they appear deflated and sheepish.)" Later Hope turns on them all. "Why don't you get the hell out of here and 'tend to your own business, like Hickey's told you?" (189). Once again, the name inspires a Beckettian reaction: "They look at him reproachfully, their eyes hurt. They fidget as if trying to move." Hickey's ensuing lines about killing pipe dreams obviously make the others want to kill him, "But they remain silent and motionless" (189). When the characters are goaded out of the bar, into the teeth of the pipe dream itself, their "action" is never completed. Hickey has shown them just how "free" they really are.

The knowledge that they are not "free," and that the struggle for self-consciousness only results in this knowledge, bleeds the characters of their social mannerisms, and they start to retreat down the evolutionary ladder. They become beasts, then automatons; they no longer want to think or feel. Of course, this undifferentiated, asocial self was a part of their social selves all along, but now it has been cut off from the differentiation, the dissimulation, the mask. There is no ironic distance between the "self" and the "history" of self. And the result is the loss of the dialectical/dialogical imperative—a loss that threatens disclosure with closure:[11] the movement away from the dialogical drama of realism and toward the monologic narrative of epic. Hickey finds himself even more in control of his imposed "narrative" than he wants to be. He becomes a single voice pitted against a chorus in act 4.

The Iceman Cometh and its bar full of has-beens with their fin-de-siècle hangovers discounts positive models of history and the possibility of social action. The social and economic strategies represented by its salesmen, gamblers, prostitutes, and anarchists are shown to be self-dramatizations, metaphors for the illusory connection between fact and fiction. The urge to make fiction fact is intoxicating; it implies power and autonomy. But this unity cannot be realized except in some self-destructive way. *The Iceman Cometh's* twin and forebear in the O'Neill canon is surely *The Hairy Ape*, in which Yank, the Neanderthal who dreams that he is power itself, the drive that runs the world, the alpha and the omega ("I'm de end! I'm de start!" *Complete Plays* 128), finds himself trapped, enslaved, and imprisoned. Yank's rise to consciousness takes the form of episodic encounters in which he loses his faith in himself as the center of the universe. When the center is lost he becomes alien to himself, a Caliban between human and beast, king and slave.

Yank is at the bottom of the scale, less than an animal, which after all "belongs" somewhere, and can, Yank imagines, at least dream of a jungle past. "But me—I ain't got no past to tink in, nor nuthin' dat's comin', on'y what's now—and dat don't belong" (162). Yank's Rodin posture becomes harder to assume, his "thinking" isolates him more and more from the civilization of which he thought (correctly, but only in a thankless economic sense) he was the driving force. Like the characters in *The Iceman Cometh*, the anarchists and petty grafters on the other side of the capitalist system, Yank realizes he is not "free." Coming out of his cave of shadows into the daylight, forced, in the Wobblies' terms, to "wake up," he finds life in "the present" to be a hazy middle ground in which his new consciousness is a kind of prison.[12] "I ain't on oith and I ain't in heaven, get me? I'm in de middle tryin' to separate 'em, takin' all de woist punches from bot' of 'em. Maybe dat's what dey call hell, huh?" (162). With the loss of the self as presence, outside his own fiction of power, Yank's play turns desperately to monologue. Without the possibility of disclosure his drama moves inexorably toward closure—and enclosure. And this is evident in the language of the play: Mildred never actually *calls* him a "hairy ape"; that is a term, and an image, that possesses *Yank* from the beginning. He is trapped by it, and it ends by defining him ("I'll show her who's a ape!" 143) The search for freedom ends in a cage; the need to belong traps him in solitary confinement; the quest for understanding becomes monologue, a doomed filibuster against death.

The epic monologue threatens, as Peter Szondi has shown, the very world on which the dialogic notion of character is based. That was a world in which the self was *reflected by* the drama, not one in which, as in epic, the character has "freedom to pause and reflect"

(Szondi 71). The very nature of the "dramatic" is thrown into relief: "the interpersonal relation becomes entirely thematic and is removed from the certainty of form to the uncertainty of content" (73). The self, in monologic (epic) theater, becomes its own object. "[T]he subject-object opposition that is at the origin of epic theater (the self-alienation of the individual, whose own social being has become reified) is precipitated formally on all levels of the work and, thus, becomes its general formal principle" (ibid.). When Hickey, like Yank, insists on taking over the play with his monologue in act 4 ("I've got to tell you!" 231), he pushes the play's form into epic monologue, just as he has been threatening to do.[13] And his monologue, like Yank's, reveals his own self-division and entraps him, denying the "freedom" on which he had based all his actions: of his dead wife, he says, "I'd have killed myself before I'd ever have hurt her!" (246). No one could put his situation more plainly.

Hickey is the ironist par excellence, who, far from demonstrating the possibility of living without the fictional or divided self, betrays, in his absolute dependence upon language, the degree of his own self-delusion and division. When Hickey realizes he has created a fiction of "Evelyn" in order to justify killing her, he concludes, necessarily, that the fiction was true and that the murder was an act of insanity—or rather, not the murder, itself, but his laughter afterward. "I remember I stood by the bed and suddenly I had to laugh. I couldn't help it. . . . You've known me longer than anyone, Harry. You know I must have been insane, don't you, Governor? . . . Yes! Or I couldn't have laughed!" (241–42). The language of irony, of the split self, does not lead here to a language that acknowledges the "inauthenticity" of the self. It leads to the "consciousness of madness," the "consciousness of a non-consciousness, a reflection on madness from the inside of madness itself" (de Man 216). And this "irony of irony" reveals its presence in laughter. Hickey laughs at Evelyn, in his confession, because in the act of killing her, he feels superior to her need for a pipe dream: "I remember I heard myself speaking to her, as if it was something I'd always wanted to say: Well, you know what you can do with your pipe dream now, you damned bitch!" (241). But he has killed her fiction of him, as well (or put another way, the absent "Evelyn" is a part of the fiction "Hickey"); and the verbal slip, like the laugh, leaves him scrambling to fill the fictive gap with another doubling, a consciousness of madness.[14] De Man finds this notion elaborated in Baudelaire's theory of laughter.

> Je ne connais guère de fous d'humilité. Remarquez que le rire est une des expressions les plus fréquentes et les plus nombreuses de la folie. . . . [Le rire] sorti des conditions fondamentales de la vie . . . est un rire qui ne dort jamais, comme une maladie qui va toujours son chemin et exécute un ordre providentiel. [Baudelaire, "De l'essence du rire," quoted in de Man 216. Alterations de Man's; he leaves the quotation untranslated]

Laughter, as Baudelaire suggests, gives the madman away, and, like the hand of fate, points a finger at his delusions of superiority. Indeed: at the moment Hickey attempts to explain his laughter as madness, Moran the detective steps forward to take him away—"Come along and spill your guts where we can get it on paper" (243). But getting it on paper will not make Hickey's doubled self any more reliable, any more unified. "You've got me all wrong, Officer," he says. "I want to go the Chair. . . . Do you suppose I give a damn about life now? Why, you bonehead, I haven't got a single damned lying hope or pipe dream left!" (245). And the play returns to its beginning, as the other characters come out of their choruslike collectivity and establish their individuality—their tales, their ironic selves—once again. "There is always," O'Neill said of *Iceman*, "one dream left" (Carpenter 149).

Hickey's intrusion has done nothing to unify "fact" with "fiction," the "self" with "the history of the self." "Far from being a return to the world, the irony to the second power or 'irony of irony' that all true irony at once has to engender asserts and maintains its fictional character by stating the continued impossibility of reconciling the world of fiction with the actual world" (de Man 218). Consciousness always makes something of experience. As consciousness, it opposes experience, the way "history" (a construction of consciousness) opposes "action" (a movement independent of this historic time consciousness and destructive of it). We never do touch reality at all points. In the structural irony of *The Iceman Cometh*, O'Neill undermines the mimetic foundation of realism. "Irony steadily undermines [the] claim at imitation and substitutes for it a conscious, interpreted awareness of the distance that separates an actual experience from the understanding of this experience" (de Man 56). Furthermore, the effect of this ironic intrusion "is not a heightened realism, an affirmation of a historical over a fictional act, but . . . has the very opposite aim and effect. . . . [T]here is no way back from [the] fictional to [the] actual self" (de Man 219).

So when Hickey is taken away, it is still not the end of the play. For the characters on stage right, the chorus, the return to "normality" is easy enough: their "characters" are always convincing, at least to themselves. But Larry and Parritt have been cut from the herd, singled out stage left, associated spatially and thematically with Hickey. Larry too thinks that he has no more interest in life, that his ironic distance from the others makes him immune to their sort of fiction, superior to them. And Parritt is a repetition of Hickey, a double Hickey dimly recognizes. ("I wish you'd get rid of that bastard, Larry. I can't have him pretending there's something in common between him and me" [227].) Hickey says he wants the Chair; Larry says he hopes death comes soon; but it is Parritt who dies in the end of the play, Parritt whose death we are waiting for.

And this is odd, because Parritt is probably the least compelling character on stage. Nobody else in the play likes him, and even by the others' standards he's a weakling, a sneak, and a coward. Hugo's name for him is telling: "leedle Don, leedle monkey-face!" Parritt is that least attractive of all characters: the self in embryo, the un-self-aware, Paleolithic self. Like the Hairy Ape, and like Hickey, Parritt is the outsider asking to be crucified, or to put it in less glorious terms, he's the character who rediscovers for the play the limits against which the apparently "limitless" extension of consciousness strives. Self-knowledge, selfhood, the freedom to act knowingly in the present, does nothing to transform the transient, material world into something human or conscious. Hickey's negation of the "false" self through gesture (as opposed to "action"), and Larry's "philosophy" of ironic detachment, his distancing of the divided selves, are seen to be half answers to the problem of "reconciling the world of fiction with the actual world" (de Man 218). It remains for Parritt to find the moment of connection between the empirical and the imagined self in their mutual destruction.

The Fall, as de Man reminds us, is a fall into the knowledge of "the reified character of [our] relation to nature" (214). "Experience" thus becomes the basis for the continual escalation of self-consciousness. But "experience" is also that which is opposed to consciousness, that which excludes it. The divided, ironic self exists in a language, to be sure, in a kind of philosophy, like Larry's, but to "progress" through such a "fall" really requires an end of consciousness. Death, like madness, then, comes like a savior and leaves like a thief: "[A]t the very moment that irony is thought of as a knowledge able to order and to cure the world, the source of its invention immediately runs dry. The instant it construes the fall of the self as an event that could somehow benefit the self, it discovers that it has in fact substituted death for madness" (de Man 218).

Parritt wants Larry to speak the word so that he can jump off the fire escape. In his position as Larry's "son" and heir, he acts out, of course, Larry's own ambivalence about death, "the movement," and Rosa Parritt, the mother/whore anarchist leader, the spirit of revolution, of action and freedom: "[S]he can't live long in jail. She loves freedom too much" (247). Parritt acts for Larry, who becomes more static and alienated from the rest of the "action" than ever as he waits for the fall. And Larry realizes that the ironic double nature he perpetuates in his language divides him from his "heart's desire." The knowledge of his doubleness can do nothing to make him a unity.

To say that we are all phonies, which would be one way to respond to this play, would be cynical—not nihilistic. Nihilism, on the other hand, is the ironic positive to cynicism's negative: to be real we have to destroy all the contingencies of a self; we have to die. But it would be naive to describe *Iceman* as nihilistic, for the unification of the heart with its desire, the destruction of those obstacles that define and isolate the self, is undramatizable. Nihilism is the ultimate romance, the permanent quest; it isn't something one *achieves*. Death, for the drama, is certainly a fiction. The point is made by Hickey's exit: he immolates himself on the altar of his imagined remorse. Parritt, however, kills himself to "get free"; his suicide is suggested as a release—he's "like a dog with its guts ripped out you'd put out of misery" (248). And Parritt's death releases *the play*: after he leaves, the drunks start to feel the kick in their drinks again.

This fall is literal, even if it is offstage, and it promises Parritt as well as the play a kind of formal integrity. That function is what makes the fall so appalling: its artificiality is so desperate; it's pathetically false. As Lionel Abel once remarked, Parritt is not only unappealing but unbelievable, undramatic. The offstage sound of his body "hurtling down, followed by a muffled, crunching thud" (257) represents O'Neill's desire for an extradramatic answer to the "now" that never arrives, the answer he had wanted at the end of The Hairy Ape: "And, perhaps, the Hairy Ape at last belongs."

4 The Glass Menagerie
Loss and Space

It's the *Gone with the Wind* of the post-World-War generation!

—Scene 3

In his film version of *The Glass Menagerie*, Paul Newman's camera moves effortlessly through the Wingfield apartment, along corridors with doors opening at the end of them into little rooms that seem to keep changing their places, out onto the landing of a fire escape. In Newman's set, unlike Williams's, the fire escape is not used for escape. Instead, a front door opens onto a staircase two flights to the ground. The fire escape remains a landing, not an exit, let alone an escape, a perch where the Wingfields hover, from which flight would seem impossible without wings. Newman has increased Williams's two rooms to eight in his film, retreating breakaway walls for the coldly lit "present" scenes. So while his camera is constantly finding other and ambiguously related spaces for the characters to inhabit, the narration in "present" time appears to be in a "future" apartment, bleak, abandoned. The déjà vu effect manages to convey three separate times into one space, as if space were symbolic of time.[1] The camera's freedom of motion through space and time is matched by Williams's own emphasis on closure and entrapment. Like the fire escape that doesn't lead anywhere, the multiple spaces created for the camera's invasion seem to cut off connections, mimicking Williams's scenic structure, which blocks off the play's events inside a fluid outer narrative. Williams himself makes the connection between realistic convention and spatial confinement: the Wingfields' tenement is

> one of those vast hive-like conglomerations of cellular living-units that flower as warty growths in overcrowded urban centers of lower middle-class population and are symptomatic of the impulse of this largest and fundamentally enslaved section

of American society to avoid fluidity and differentiation and to exist and function as one interfused mass of automatism. [143]

The cells are "symptomatic" of an "impulse" to "exist" and "function"—the analytical language of observable instincts would have the middle class playing right into the hands of realistic drama, where they could be studied naturalistically, as a "hive" or "warty growth" without "fluidity and differentiation," the unifying impulse an attempt to avoid difference, as if these connecting cells were a single organism. Any part of such an organism could then be detached and studied as the representative of the whole and without any damage to the rest; each segment would corroborate its neighbor. The tenement thus represents the opposite of "truth" (which is Williams's word for "reality," as it was Chekhov's): that which manifests itself through difference and dissimulation— "transformation," Williams calls it (131), "changing into other forms than those which were merely present in appearance." The notion of drama as transformation, a moving perspective, makes meaning a matter not of consistency, but of montage, a spatialized time that sees via juxtaposition rather than persistence of vision. Like a film, the scenic structure blocks off events that depend on contiguity rather than continuity.

Film's impact on stage imaging must have been enormous and contradictory: technological advances in the reproduction and recapturing of the image had the potential both to minimize and to magnify drama's optical effects. By the time he wrote *The Glass Menagerie*, and despite the rapid development of film technique in the twenties and thirties, Williams could claim that "[e]veryone should know nowadays the unimportance of the photographic in art" (131). Like O'Neill, who disparaged realism as the "family Kodak," Williams seems to use the word "photographic" as a synonym for realistic. Photography and film are difficult to separate as influences, and indeed Williams's play seems ambivalent about them both. The movies and the photograph are central to *Glass Menagerie*'s mise-en-scène, alike for their power to image and for their power to expose the image's boundaries in space and time. Realism's barriers stand at the threshold of a spatial/temporal unity that is supposed to be absolute; but the optical effect is really, as Einstein showed, a kind of defect, an illusion that, as Williams says of the (realistic) theater, has the appearance of truth (144). The key to the appearance of simultaneity, to the persistence of vision and its promise of the unbroken, unmediated image, was movement—distance, velocity, and in film editing, projection (which includes the speed of the film), the opening and closing of the shutter. Not surprisingly, Brecht saw film technique as a tool for the destruction of "static" Aristotelian or mimetic theater. "For the film the principles of non-aristotelian drama (a type of drama not depending on empathy, mimesis) are immediately acceptable" (50). Piscator's use of projections and revolving stages gave the Lehrstück a greater range of social commentary; they also gave it movement: "The learning-play is essentially dynamic; its task is to show the world as it changes (and also how it may be changed)" (79). For Brecht the change did not occur in the dark, in an Augenblick, a moment between moments, a winking of the eye, but was a part—the most important part—of the dramatic content.

Brecht is aware that film technique breaks down the sanctity of the image, its elevation to the uses of "free-floating contemplation" (Benjamin 226). "[The film] apparatus can be used better than almost anything else to supersede the old kind of un-technical, antitechnical 'glowing' art, with its religious links" (Brecht 48). At the same time, Brecht recognizes the capitalist permeation of film production, and likewise Benjamin points out the film industry's commodification of the image, with its fascist implications. The power of film to break barriers of virtual presence corresponds to its uses for invasion, mobilization in both its general and technical senses, and capitulation.

Williams creates and dissolves scenic barriers in The Glass Menagerie with titles, music, and lighting; he calls attention to his editorial technique. There is a blackout as each scene changes; music cues ends and beginnings or, as in scenes 1 and 2, bridges the action over the blackout. Title or image projections create moments within a scene, underlining (and so of course ironizing, not ironing out) the dramatic structure. The incongruity of the stills in the midst of a scene has a ridiculous effect, the way the titles in a silent movie sometimes do. This doesn't make them "undramatic." The absurd, as Chekhov has demonstrated, can cohabit with the poignant; it may even have its own poignancy. Williams seems to think the titles necessary in a more "fluid" play, because he knows the audience is used to a stable perspective.

> Each scene contains a particular point (or several) which is structurally the most important. In an episodic play, such as this, the basic structure or narrative line may be obscured from the audience; the effect may seem fragmentary rather than architectural. This may not be the fault of the play so much as a lack of attention in the audience. [132]

Williams wants to make his points "simply and lightly" so the "spoken lines" won't carry such a weight of "responsibility." But the titles were not used in the original production, *The Glass Menagerie* is often given a realistic mise-en-scène, and the play's dialogue, perhaps bearing out Williams's apprehensions, is sometimes criticized for sounding weakly sentimental.

The suggestion that dialogue carries too much weight in the theater, however, as Artaud has shown, importantly implies a new sense of value for the mise-en-scène. Indeed one could say that projecting language on a screen alternated with projected images makes language part of the mise-en-scène, not a higher form of expression. At the same time, the projections call attention to language and mise-en-scène in a new way, with a now-you-see-it-now-you-don't illusion. As Williams envisions them, they appear at seemingly random moments on a particular wall and then disappear again into the set. "These images and legends, projected from behind, were cast on a section of wall between the front-room and dining-room areas, which should be indistinguishable from the rest when not in use" (132). Thus the projections never quite disappear into the pattern of the play, because they occur sporadically and because they keep taking over a portion of the "realistic" setting. Yet Williams apparently assumes they will have their impact on feeling as much as thought. "Aside from this structural value, I think the screen will have a definite emotional appeal, less definable but just as important" (132). It is typical of Williams to describe what some people might call an alienation effect in emotional terms—art itself has emotional value for him, as if it were some frail creature destined for extinction. The possibility of art's destruction is represented throughout *Glass Menagerie* by the shattering of glass (sc. 3, 164; sc. 7,

225–26, 236). It is as close as the Wingfields come to experiencing the "bombardments" that were "imminent in this year" (179).

The titles in *Glass Menagerie* do indeed have "epic" effect: they create a third term of reference outside character and mise-en-scène necessary for montage (cf. Szondi 76), and as part of the mise-en-scène they, as Szondi says of the epic stage, quote, anticipate, and remind rather than represent (72). Brecht, moreover, like Williams, stressed the emotional content in epic's apparent rationalism.

> It is not true, though it is sometimes suggested, that epic theatre (which is not simply undramatic theatre, as is also sometimes suggested) proclaims the slogan: "Reason this side, Emotion (feeling) that." It by no means renounces emotion. . . . The "attitude of criticism" which it tries to awaken in its audience cannot be passionate enough for it. [Brecht 227]

It is hard to imagine that Williams had anything else in mind for the "emotional appeal" of his screens, which often seem to parody the play's action and certainly its dialogue. (Is it any wonder that Tom is always *smoking*, an attitude—perhaps more than a practice—Amanda detests?)

"Ou sont les neiges" [sic] one of the first screens asks, as Amanda goes into her "gentleman caller" routine. She speaks to Tom, who is standing by the portieres, as though he were still at the table. Tom plays this scene, Williams says, "as though reading from a script."

TOM: I know what's coming!
LAURA: Yes. But let her tell it.
TOM: Again?
LAURA: She loves to tell it.
[147]

The scene has already been announced as "Ou sont les neiges" (146), so we are ready for something like this. But the image of blue roses that opens scene 2 is unreadable until nearly the scene's end, and gradually, for a little while, the legends/images almost achieve perfect simultaneity with the script, as if to punctuate the dialogue (155, 192, 196). The screen seems to have its own logic, running parallel to the action but not quite in sync with it. Often it points ahead or makes an allusion in the dialogue literal—more or less the way the father's photograph seems literally to *be* he at times, commenting on the dialogue or receiving its messages.

The characters are often treated as images, themselves, creatures inhabiting another artistic space not of the mise-en-scène. The lighting isolates Laura (sc. 3, sc. 7) and Amanda (sc. 4). Williams describes the desired effect: "Shafts of light are focused on selected areas or actors, sometimes in contradistinction to what is the apparent center. . . . A certain correspondence to light in religious paintings, such as El Greco's, where the figures are radiant in atmosphere that is relatively dusky, could be effectively used throughout the play" (133–34). That the framing device also heightens the image for Williams, creating the effect found in Renaissance religious painting, is a reminder of the lost ritual value of the image with the advent of mechanical reproduction. "The secular cult of beauty, developed during the Renaissance and prevailing for three centuries, clearly showed that ritualistic basis in its decline and the first deep crisis which befell it" (Benjamin 224). The effect of the "El Greco" lighting on the image is referential, ritualistic, aware of the lost perception it evokes. Williams's iconic imagery measures the loss with an absurdly tragic intensity. Similarly, in *Portrait of a Madonna*, a one-act that seems to have been a study for *Streetcar*, a spinster named Lucretia Collins goes mad, imagining that her long lost beau breaks into her apartment every night and rapes her. Her passion is expressed by the overpowering desecration of the sacred image in an ironic scenario of loss and restoration.

As in cinema, the lighting creates shadings of space within the larger space of the scene and the action, a recentering that enables the play's perspective to move, subjectively zooming in or highlighting features, as when Amanda's are made "sharp" and "satirical as a Daumier print" (sc. 4). Williams is aware of the cinematic mobile illusion of his lighting: "A free, imaginative use of light can be of enormous value in giving a mobile, plastic quality to plays of a more or less static nature" (134). Jo Mielziner, who designed the sets for *Glass Menagerie*, *A Streetcar Named Desire*, and other first productions of Williams's plays, found in Williams an "instinct" for visual movement. "If he had written plays in the days before the technical development of translucent and transparent scenery, I believe he would have invented it" (124).

The delicate reframing within scenes is itself part of a larger continual reframing that breaks down, as Newman tries to do with his camera, the totality of the set. At first, a realistic, even naturalistic setting seems to define the play's field of action:

> The apartment faces an alley and is entered by a fire escape, a structure whose name is a touch of accidental poetic truth, for all of these huge buildings are always burning with the slow and implacable fires of human desperation.

> At the rise of the curtain, the audience is faced with the dark, grim rear wall of the Wingfield tenement. This building is flanked on both sides by dark, narrow alleys which run into murky canyons of tangled clotheslines, garbage cans, and the sinister latticework of neighboring fire escapes. [143]

Williams has written expressly for a proscenium stage and sets the play smack in the middle of realism's messy continuous recognizable world. A curtain rises. And then the set is revealed as another curtain: "At the end of Tom's opening commentary, the dark tenement wall slowly becomes transparent and reveals the interior of the ground-floor Wingfield apartment" (143). Finally, a third curtain separates the audience from the action of the first scene. "The audience hears and sees the opening scene in the dining room through both the transparent fourth wall of the building and the transparent gauze portieres of the dining-room arch" (144). Again the ritualistic hiddenness of the image that promises its uniqueness is laid bare by the film technique, an optical intrusion of distance effected by the stripping away of multiple curtains. The image keeps receding, past the fourth wall that has been made visible, into the depths of another picture, framed by the dining room arch and fifth wall or defining plane between living room and dining room.

The effect is extraordinary, like deep focus in cinema, a technique Welles had recently explored in *Citizen Kane* (1941). There, the first sequence about young Charles shows him playing with his sled in the snow and then pulls back to the inside of a window through which his parents and his new guardian are watching, then back into the room and further yet into an adjoining room beyond. In this unusual tracking shot, the characters follow the camera rather than the reverse and seem to be invading its space, constantly forcing it to step back from a new perspective. The camera creates continuity between scenes in a new way, without editing, and unites symbolically elements of the narrative that would otherwise have to be divided or juxtaposed by montage. But this continuity is also achieved by breaking down the framing, the perspective, at each remove, reinventing the scene (is it going to be about Charles? is it going to be about his parents?) and the spatial "illusion." The spatial relativity here in fact seems to be pulling the narrative along with it: we don't know what the narrative is until we know where we are in the "scene." We need to keep refocusing, as our eyes do anyway, but now, consciously, the way cinematographers had to keep altering the focus of their lenses before the availability of deep focus technology.

Structures of meaning in the visual narrative are built up and broken down, and the broken sense of scale and distance makes the pieces seem incommensurate, as if no model (idea) can be made of them: *Citizen Kane*'s famous image of a jigsaw puzzle with missing pieces. Oddly, the unimpeded movement of the camera beyond the framed space creates a sense of dislocation, an infinitely revisable narrative, even as it serves the desire for unity by obviating the need for editing. Outside a lost organicism, form is imitated by the power of regeneration. The organic unity of naturalism is replaced by the cinema's endlessly reproducible images. Only live organisms, Susanne Langer writes, "strive to achieve [forms]" and "maintain themselves in them" (89): life develops and matures in an organic and orderly way. Everything else is oblivious to form—unless it is capable of self-regeneration.

> Other accretions of matter may have *usual* forms, but do not strive to achieve them, nor maintain themselves in them. A crystal broken in half yields simply two pieces of crystal. A creature broken in half either dies, i.e. disintegrates, or repairs one part, or both parts, to function again as a whole. It may even break just because the new wholes are preformed, the repair all but made, so the break is its dynamic pattern. [89]

The need to reimagine wholeness through what is broken is thus a kind of dividing line between art and organicism. In *The Glass Me-*

nagerie broken crystal has two related meanings: rupture and the return to normalcy. "I'll just imagine he had an operation," Laura says of her unicorn, who has been broken precisely at his horn, his extra appendage. "The horn was removed to make him feel less—freakish! . . . Now he will feel more at home with the other horses, the ones that don't have horns" (226). Normalcy here is an affectation of wholeness, making the best of a break that can't be repaired, of pieces that can't be put together again. Similarly, in realism what is "well made" is a recognizable form that answers a desire for unity; realistic form fulfills an anxiety for realism, providing perhaps "a certain amount of comfort" (Lyotard 76).

Throughout the play Tom's narrative posture divides him from the spatial-temporal world he is "remembering." But he cannot release himself from it at will; "the play" has to break itself off from him ("Blow out your candles, Laura"). The broken image repairs the anxiety for form, closure, resolution—it's a consolation prize. Representation when it imitates organicism is a consoling image of regeneration and endlessly available normalcy. We are reformed into our stable perspective. Thus for Williams the real curtain signaling the beginning and end of the play is the fourth wall, realism's defining plane. "It is during this revealing scene [scene 1] that the fourth wall slowly ascends, out of sight. This transparent exterior wall is not brought down again until the very end of the play, during Tom's final speech" (144). The controlling apparatus of the fourth wall and its normalizing trick of perspective creates the illusion of truth—"Illusion that has the appearance of truth," Tom calls the magic of the "stage magician" (144). "Malvolio the Magician" has a magic scarf: "You wave it over a canary cage and you get a bowl of goldfish. You wave it over the goldfish bowl and they fly away canaries" (167). It is yet another curtain. The revelation is magic, that optical illusion.

The plastic theater Williams envisions suggests multiple perspectives, a relative space-time relationship, that breaks the temporal hold on the form as causal, chronological, continuous. "In a play, time is arrested in the sense of being confined. By a sort of legerdemain, events are made to remain *events*, rather than being reduced so quickly to mere *occurrences*" (Williams II, 261). This spatial treatment of time permits the "contemplative" suspension of it and enables the playwright to hold and measure the value of word or gesture. Such a measure is suggested by classical rules of scale and proportion. Beauty is for Aristotle "bound up with size and order" (*On the Art of Poetry* 42). The time it takes to see something, and the time it can be held in the memory, are to determine its size and duration: "A minutely small creature, therefore, would not be beautiful, for it would take almost no time to see it and our perception of it would be blurred; . . . [S]o too plots must be of a reasonable length, so that they may be easily held in the memory" (42). The effort here is to create, not just a whole thing with a beginning, middle and end, a logical or "probable" order, but something that can be perceived as a unity, a semblance of wholeness that must not be "lost to the view of the beholder" (ibid.).

The perception of unity, however, presupposes that the perceiver looks *beyond* the creature and its plot to a vision of order with which she started; in Brecht's terms, one's "eyes [are] on the finish" (37). The starting point of the perception of order is understood in Aristotle, which is to say that it is culturally defined: "The human being is taken for granted" (Brecht 37). Thus the art is already establishing its perceptual difference on a sameness, a notion clearly implied in Langer's definitions of "virtual space"—on the one hand, not connected to experiential space (72), yet inventing "a space whereof [the human] is the center" (90), a culturally defined space (95), a space creating semblances of "a self-contained, total system" (75). In a painting, Langer says, we look past the picture's defining plane toward the "virtual space" it represents. In sculpture, space is organized in three dimensions to represent, not a scene, but an organism: "It is *virtual kinetic volume*, created by—and with—the semblance of living form" (89). In architecture, a "virtual place" is created in an "actual place"; the spectator recognizes an "ethnic domain," a perceptual space of a "cultural," a "geographical semblance" (95). The language of "non-discursive" art, whether two- or three-dimensional, is for Langer a "logic . . . all of a piece" (103). The human/organic premises of this system Langer is quick to point out, but they lead her to the curious assertion that "plastic form" is *not* an important concept in theater or ballet, where there is no evident attempt at "creating space" (103).

Some assumptions about representation emerge from Aristotle's and Langer's sense of scale, space, and duration. Representation, as Langer puts it, "is for the sake of creating individual forms in visible relation to one another" (76). Here "for the sake of" points our eyes toward the finish, while the notion of "visible relation" suggests the way we are invited to see semblances. We are to look beyond the scene to its purpose and to perceive its purposive unity through spatial relationships.

> "The space of which we are clearly conscious when we attend to [the surface, the 'picture plane'] lies behind it. It commences with the plane." (Langer 78, quoting Adolf Hildebrand, *The Problem of Form in Painting and Sculpture*)

> The space itself is a projected image, and everything pictured serves to define and organize it. [Langer 77]

The human-centered perception of Langer and Aristotle assumes too a placement of the perceiver: she can never move from that point, which makes her the object of her own perception. She supplies the organizing principle and the vantage point that defines the principle in the first place. This perceiver can only *be moved* (i.e., psychologically or emotionally affected) through empathy with the object of her perception. Realistic representation makes such an empathy axiomatic, as Brecht observed, since the point of the representation is to create an illusory identity between the subject and its object. Aristotelian aesthetics is strongly tied to Aristotelian physics: anthropomorphic and goal-centered (Bernstein 24), it subjects all motion to a law of gravitational identity. The subject's displacement is scarcely hypothesized, for there is no point at which the subject's perception is not reflecting her own perception of unity. The vision of realistic drama is thus the vision of the unified object, made identifiable with the subject through an erasure of its defining space. Space is totalized, infinite, a vision of self-as-world synecdochically symbolized by the mise-en-scène—"the semblance of that World which is the counterpart of a Self" (Langer 98). Realism looks past the apparatus of the theater and creates the illusion that the spectator, not the apparatus, controls that look. It may be that there is no logical way to assume the "stab[le] referent" (Lyotard 74) without assuring the stability of the spectator. In this sense, realistic perspective looks back from the form to the observed observer, not mimetically imaged by the form exactly but thrown back by the form into an image of itself. That is perhaps why Lyotard sees realism as a kind of tacit collective control (74) playing directly to a desire of realism that is also "a desire for unity" (73).

With its erasure of space realism presents an absolute time, a present that seems fixed, via *simultaneity*. The mise-en-scène, which in classical drama was a backdrop for the dialogue, becomes itself a character—or at least it is prior to and after Expressionism, where mise-en-scène was perhaps perceived as too powerful, too "in-human," in the sense that it did not "serve" the human ends, an idea to which we will return in the next chapter. The set and dialogue are mutually supportive in realism, mutually creative, and thus (as we saw in chapter 2) "revealing" of character. Spatial divisions in realistic sets suggest not just a character's milieu but in fact her *psychology*, since the realistic plot relies on anxiety rather than action for its suspense (sense of duration). Closure is necessary as the relief from anxiety. The "anxiety" is an incompleteness of knowledge, a felt suppression that is really a secret screaming to get out of formal constraints that are thus made to seem actual. The form is the suspense of the secret. Everything must serve to reinforce the logic of the form—dialogue, set, and movement must be a seamless web from which secrecy, like Malvolio the magician, must seem to struggle to escape. "But the wonderfullest trick of all was the coffin trick. We nailed him into a coffin and he got out of the coffin without removing one nail" (167). As realism develops in the modern period, the formal process of disclosure becomes more and more apparent, until finally everything in the theatrical space seems charged with intersubjectivity. Chekhov, for example, has a character who makes a lengthy speech to a bookcase.

The formal anxiety of realism is created, however, not only by the reinforcement of the verbal by the visual, the mimetic reciprocity of dialogue and mise-en-scène, but also by the powerful inexpressiveness of the set. It represents the finality of objects, of objectivity. This simultaneous expression of and indifference to human psychology is the effect of objectified space and time, which seem "objective" only because they can be corroborated. "Objective" time "is, in reality, a statement about the simultaneous occurrence of two events" (Bernstein 58); in other words, the problem of a mimetic effect depends upon a temporal-spatial concept of comparison and corroboration, between text and stage image as well as between the "present" onstage and another present that exists "elsewhere and prior to it" (Derrida, *Writing and Difference* 237). The objectivity of the drama is established by an imaginary spatial-temporal referent, a referent that is thus entirely susceptible to collective control.

"Time" cannot enter the simultaneous events of realistic drama except as psychological progression. "To give a simple definition, a length [of plot] which, as a matter either of probability or necessity, allows of a change from misery to happiness or from happiness to misery is the proper limit of length to be observed" (Aristotle, *On the Art of Poetry* 42). The play is simultaneous with the imagined present, its duration represented by the time covered between two comparative psychological states. Perceiving time as the motion between two mutually exclusive emotional positions is the first thing that Williams, like Chekhov, rejects: emotions and so goals and progress toward them are difficult to fix.

> AMANDA: Now! Now, darling, wish!
> LAURA: What shall I wish for, Mother?
> AMANDA: (her voice trembling and her eyes suddenly filling with tears)
> Happiness! Good fortune!
> [189]

> AMANDA: You are the only young man that I know of who ignores the fact that the future becomes the present, the present the past, and the past turns into everlasting regret if you don't plan for it!
> TOM: I will think that over and see what I can make of it.
> [185]

The emotional progress of the plot is impossible to measure when past, present, and future "become" one another in Amanda's line, which seems so to echo Mary in *Long Day's Journey*. Williams's lines show how the temporal spacing gets flattened out, how one temporality all at once "turns into" the next. To break up spatial-temporal simultaneity, time would have to be able to enter the play. Not that the play could ever enter historical time: that, as we have seen in the preceding chapter, is impossible. But a sense of time can be built into the play, presumably, through the wounding of space and the intervention of time: "The diminishing influence of life's destroyer, time, must be somehow worked into the context of [the] play" (Williams II, 263). And this reopening of space from inside its structure, no longer an "objective" fixing of experience, must consequently refuse to corroborate a present or a psychology of anxiety and closure. The vantage point of the audience has to be unfixed, which means that the play must continually move without trying necessarily to "move."

Williams's invasion of realism's space occurs just through his strategy of working time into the play. "The play is memory." Tom's opening speech in The Glass Menagerie explains the break with realism in ambiguous terms. "[I]t is dimly lighted, it is sentimental, it is not realistic. In memory everything seems to happen to music. That explains the fiddle in the wings" (145). The effect here may seem, on the face of the page, to settle the audience into a comfortable, child-like coziness of warmth and illusion. But the announcement of its sentimentality is, one may say, really the opposite of sentimentality, unless we were allowed to forget about this commenting voice for the rest of the play. Williams, however, takes care to remind us of the play's historical relativism. Tom's opening speech itself includes an analysis of The Glass Menagerie's social and historical setting: this is a forties play written about the thirties ("To begin with, I turn back time" [145]). The failing economy, the rise of fascism, revolution in Spain and labor protests in the United States are "the social background of the play." Hints of impending disaster, of the strong triumphing over the weak, of time as a destroyer, are periodically reinforced (178, 179; 201), notably in the play's closing lines.

At the same time the ambiguity of the final speech, which is about an image attempting to break (from) another image, suggests spatial relativity: images won't take their turn, or stay where they belong. Through an associative freedom of motion, Williams's verbal and visual images clash with and reflect one another, continually shifting space and time perspectives. The historical references fix the play's events, but the unfixing of time's control over events gives space a new voice. Time is distance. Space is thus able to break free of its representational constraints, free to evoke time. And what is "memory" if not the ability to image time?

Language, too, set free by mechanical powers of reproduction and transmission, establishes at once farther reaching and more tenuous connections, intruding through time and space far more audaciously even than the printed word. Here is Amanda selling subscriptions to *The Homemaker's Companion*:

> You remember how *Gone with the Wind* took everybody by storm? You simply couldn't go out if you hadn't read it. All everybody *talked* was Scarlett O'Hara. Well, this is a book that critics already compare to *Gone with the Wind*. It's the *Gone with the Wind* of the post-World-War generation!—What?—Burning?—Oh, honey, don't let them burn, go take a look in the oven and I'll hold the wire! Heavens—I think she's hung up! [160]

The images overlap without really connecting; the telephone, seeming to eliminate distance, creates a comic one. "Dialogue," having lost its respondent, becomes monologue (in an obvious set piece), emphasizing arbitrary and so breakable connections. Within the setting of the "post-World-War" era, Amanda's reference to *Gone with the Wind* supplies an association of images that ends by breaking the connection. The power of the call to recall is extensive, propulsive; the incongruities seem to invent new creative associations between wars and their texts, Amanda as a 1944 Scarlett—"What?—Burning?—Oh, honey, don't let them burn." It is as if the comparison with Scarlett and Atlanta had spontaneously combusted.

The participant narrator establishes other more dangerous incongruities. Like Newman's practice of retreating and relighting the same set to suggest a future (present) for the narration, the narrator's "separate point in time and space" (133) displaces and estranges the play from itself. The setting is familiar yet unknowable, "sentimental" yet critically aware of its sentimentality in "that quaint period, the thirties, when the huge middle class of America was matriculating in a school for the blind" (145). Arguably the most brutal scenes occur in the Gentleman Caller sequence that ends the play (sc. 5–7). The long-dreamed-of Jim (the only character in the play who attends school) is announced, arrives, and leaves but not before Laura has a fit of panic, the lights go out, the favorite piece of the glass menagerie is broken, and Amanda and Tom have their last—and least comic—argument. "Don't think about us, a mother deserted, an unmarried sister who's crippled and has no job! Don't let anything interfere with your selfish pleasure!" (236). These scenes also contain the play's most explicit references to war and fascism. Tom is discovered in scene 5 reading a newspaper with the headline "Franco Triumphs." From his narrative position outside the scene Tom can see the cataclysmic changes to come, "Suspended in the mist over Berchtesgaden, caught in the folds of Chamberlain's umbrella" (179). Other implications of breakup and selfish destruction are transmitted through the portrait of the absent father, not dead, just wandering, the "fifth character in the play" to whose "larger-than-life-size photograph"—in World War I uniform—the others often refer. The "telephone man who fell in love with long distances" doesn't have a story, a reason, an ostensible goal. His last communication is a postcard: " 'Hello—Goodbye!' and no address" (145). He is just a lost connection, a broken line of meaning and communication. Yet his smiling carefree image won't go away, "as if to say, 'I will be smiling forever' " (144). It's another frozen image of time, both past and to come. The picture's presence in the scene thus underscores the father's distance: "for time is the longest distance between two places" (236).[2]

The alienating effects of technology—the telephone for example as an ultimate distance and a broken connection—make it possible to contemplate war as a desired consummation, a consummation of desire.[3] It is fitting that the Gentleman Caller who "believes in the future of television" and fascism arrive as if on the same cue. War is one way of eliminating a kind of longing for closeness, for someone or something to arrive at last.

> [T]he orchestra played a waltz or a tango, something that had a slow and sensuous rhythm. Couples would come outside, to the relative privacy of the alley. You could see them kissing behind ash pits and telephone poles. This was the compensation for lives that passed like mine, without any change or adventure. Adventure and change were imminent in this year. They were waiting around the corner for all these kids. . . . In Spain there was Guernica! But here there was only hot swing music

and liquor, dance halls, bars, and movies, and sex that hung in the gloom like a chandelier and flooded the world with brief, deceptive rainbows. . . . All the world was waiting for bombardments! [179]

Tom delivers this speech while Amanda stands looking at the father's World War I photograph, to music of "The World Is Waiting for the Sunrise!" Fascism is a total technological mobilization and a movement of the masses who go to movies from a craving for movement.

> You know what happens? People go to the *movies* instead of *moving!* Hollywood characters are supposed to have all the adventures for everybody in America, while everybody in America sits in a dark room and watches them have them! Yes, until there's a war. That's when adventure becomes available to the masses! *Everyone's* dish, not only Gable's! [201]

Like O'Neill in *Iceman*, Williams represents a U.S. culture caught in an existential freeze frame, and he is just as worried about the possibilities for remedy. "Fascism . . . expects war to supply the artistic gratification of a sense perception that has been changed by technology" (Benjamin 242). Nor do alterations in the technology of communication admit of retreat. "For the old forms of communication are not unaffected by the development of new ones, nor do they survive alongside them. The filmgoer develops a different way of reading stories. But the man who writes the stories is a filmgoer too. The mechanization of literary production cannot be thrown into reverse" (Brecht 47).

Film narrative alters the desire for reality and the writing of realism. The associativeness of the "memory play" intrudes on "objective time" by emphasizing time's relativity to space, simultaneously representing at least two images of temporality. In realism time is objectified by the presumption of the image's simultaneous corroboration, a consensus "of what exists" (Lyotard 74). But here that space is traveled, reproducing the process of comparison in unstable images, where the fixing of an image by another image is seen in all its arbitrariness. Well, not quite arbitrariness; but the imaginary control of a "subjective" narrative perspective (whatever that may be) is hardly reassuring. The narrative frame of *The Glass Menagerie* puts the entire play into memory, a radical expressionism without limits. What Peter Szondi has said of Miller's "memory" technique in *Death of a Salesman* is even truer of *The Glass Menagerie*:

> The dramatic unities are likewise abolished—indeed, abolished in the most radical sense: memory signifies not only a multiplicity of times and places but also the absolute loss of their identity. The temporal-spatial present of the action is not simply relativized in terms of other presents; on the contrary, it is in itself relative. Therefore, there is no real change in the setting, and, at the same time, it is perpetually transformed. [93–94]

Szondi might have gone further: even the means of determining change has been lost in some real sense, since no state of mind can be seen as originary. Thus the transformation can be affirmed only in its process, not in its effects. The temporal ordering of mimesis having been relativized radically, its power to stabilize the image is revealed as coercive force. The Einsteinian relativity of time to space is actually denied by realism; time is superior to space in realism's conceptual hierarchy, where the options must be left open for a return to the mimetic referent, to the contemplation of an anterior reality, a genesis. The *space* of drama seems, or rather is of course *meant* to seem, arbitrary, a territory that comes with the principle, to reverse the common saying. The bourgeois or working-class setting, the family or urban milieu, is understood as standing in place of a totality, but it is also a part of that totality. The space of realism is synecdochic of a larger space of which it is "a slice"—a neatly sectioned radius representing on its own an organic whole, not an oddly shaped fragment from a puzzle. The point is to be able to infer the whole from its part, or put another way, the part is an imitation of its whole, in small.

On the other hand, then, the space of realism cannot seem (merely) arbitrary; it has to seem to have a necessary connection to its referent, has to in fact seem to blend with it, beyond the wings. The realistic setting is understood as a segmented space whose arbitrariness is evidence of its system: any random test will produce an apparent order. Space remains static, keeps its place, cannot move. Motion is the prerogative of time. Time, as the originating impulse for mimetic order, is disassociated from spatial consideration and elevated above it, precisely to avoid relativity in the "simple, economic geometry of a 'house of certainty' " (Foucault, *Discipline* 202). Of "this devaluation of space that has prevailed for generations," Foucault writes: "Space was treated as the dead, the fixed, the undialectical, the immobile. Time, on the contrary, was richness, fecundity, life, dialectic" (Foucault, *Power/Knowledge* 70). For these reasons, perhaps, political and economic theories that posit a "change" from a "present" reality must privilege time (Foucault, *Power/Knowledge* 76). Meanwhile the segmentation of space was exploited in the capitalist era of population explosion and distributed labor, when it was necessary to discipline bodies in order to accumulate wealth (Foucault, *Discipline* 220–21). The effort to represent an evolutionary, organic, "living continuity" is an effort directed against the primacy of spatial concepts. It creates a gap between the relativistic space-time coordinates, a war from political motives. "If one started to talk in terms of space that meant one was hostile to time. It meant, as the fools say, that one 'denied history,' that one was a 'technocrat' " (Foucault, *Power/Knowledge* 70).

Nevertheless with the inclusion of the spatial synecdoche as an equal partner in its representational process, realism can be seen to acquire a new insidiousness of territorial obsession. For realism at its most sophisticated complicates the spatial relationships within the synecdochic space. It wages territorial wars over space, makes the domination of space seem to reflect the play's anxiety; whereas this domination turns out to be the anxiety's true *object*. The parallel opposing figures and dialogical form represent conflict as psychological, but it is really literally the *space* represented that is at stake, not some issue or moral principle. The struggle in *A Doll House*, for example, might appear to be Nora's will versus Torvald's concern for propriety, as represented by the forgery, the parallel figures of Kristine and Krogstad, and so forth. But the conflict can also be seen as a struggle to obtain domination of the domicile, where the male is culturally in control. Note too that Mrs. Tanqueray is always in her play a displaced person, as is Hedda Gabler, who retreats further and further until she can retreat no more—she hides behind the curtain to shoot herself.[4]

The spatial differentiation of realistic character marks off territories in deference to the characters' psychological positions—or actually the characters are defined and limited by their spatial positionings, sitting by the stove, looking out the window, pacing nervously around the room. The embattled character of the woman seeks shelter offstage—"Visibility is a trap," as Foucault says (Foucault, *Discipline* 200). There is a clear complicity, then, between realistic spacing and gender definition. Both stand firmly on the side—on the ground—of "the historical" so as to obscure its spatial categories. Not that the relationship of character to mise-en-scène remains static: the hidden logic of realistic spacing depends rather on the stability of the spectator, who sees the territorial objectives of the male and female characters via a defining cultural principle and who identifies masculine and feminine by recognizing their relative positionings. The realistic drama creates a stable point of view that it seems also to assume in its audience.

The defining and confining power of realistic space establishes a firm order in which the anxiety of the drama can be expressed, explained, and closed off. This analytical order is the antithesis of "the plague": "Against the plague, which is a mixture, discipline brings into play its power, which is one of analysis" (Foucault, *Discipline* 197). This notion, that the motive of spatial confinement and analysis lies in the anxiety of disorder, will seem even clearer in *A Streetcar Named Desire*. Individuation, of character and territory, seeming like psychological exploration, liberal and liberating, is also a powerful prescription for (and of) paranoia—using "procedures of individualization to mark exclusion" (Foucault, *Discipline* 199).

The image of analytical space is Bentham's Panopticon. Foucault notes the dramatic implications of its cells—"so many small theatres" (Foucault, *Discipline* 200)—that enhance the relative power relationship of seer-seen through cleverly compartmentalized spaces. Space is as it were rendered invisible by this process, because the Panopticon's aim is as its name suggests the construction of the observed observer, the uninterrupted illusion of a mutual gaze: "The panoptic mechanism arranges spatial unities that make it possible to see constantly and to recognize immediately" (Foucault, *Discipline* 200). The illusion of panopticism must necessarily be a constant: not a perception or a perspective but a theoretically unbroken vision. When all spaces are visible, there is nowhere to hide. Light shines in everywhere. Vision is king. But those who are being seen, the creatures in the "theatres," cannot be sure where or when the supervisor is seeing them, so they must assume a constant visibility that is only theoretically, virtually possible.

Is it far from this assumption to Langer's "virtual space" and the spatial analysis of realism, with its illusion of visual continuity? If the visibility allowed a break, the simultaneity of vision-comparison would be interrupted, causing a disjuncture within the mimetic illusion. The illusion of total and uninterrupted visibility—which means the transparency of its spatial analysis—would have to be maintained for realism's "recognition" to be "immediate." But the persistence and relentlessness of visibility has yet another relation to spatial analysis, namely, study. Recognition is helped on by the system of classification: a hint of the origins of realistic staging in the science of naturalism. Realism studies the organism in its habitat and identifies its species' properties. Confinement is analogous to classification; it is not just a convenience.

Williams seems aware of naturalism's classifying impulses in *The Glass Menagerie*: the flat is part of a large, impersonal tenement, "symptomatic" of middle-class aspirations; Laura is "the type" of woman "people call home girls" (174). References to animals and animality are constant, beginning in scene 1 with Amanda's comparison of Tom to animals with "secretions in their stomachs which enable them to digest food without mastication" (146). Moreover, science's explanations imply an insidious will to mastery: technology is associated with power and capitalism in Jim's comic equation: "Because I believe in the future of television! . . . *Knowledge*—Zzzzzp! *Money*—Zzzzzzp!—*Power*! That's the cycle democracy is built on!" (222). Television, telephone, telegraph, and radio, like film, answer a mass desire for closeness and excitement. It is as if, destroying the aura of the image, technology had created its own aura. "AMANDA: Isn't electricity a mysterious thing? Wasn't it Benjamin Franklin who tied a key to a kite? We live in such a mysterious universe, don't we? Some people say that science clears up all the mysteries for us. In my opinion it only creates more!" (208).[5] Amanda's sense of mystery does not, however, immunize her from the power of realistic analysis; on the contrary she is herself a character in imminent danger of classification. Williams's production notes warn against this: "Her characterization must be carefully created, not copied from type. She is not paranoiac, but her life is paranoia" (129). The very process of her representation and individuation risks marking Amanda for exclusion.

The menagerie collects the elements of realistic space into an image ("an ornament"): scale, transparency, animality, naturalist science. "Little articles of it, they're ornaments mostly! Most of them are little animals made out of glass, the tiniest little animals in the world. Mother calls them a glass menagerie!" (222). As the word "articles" suggests, the menagerie's creatures are too small to be seen distinctly—they are imaged really through language—indeed what is most striking about the image of the menagerie is its inessential quality, its lack of substance. "Hold him over the light! . . . You see how the light shines through him?" (223). Lest we miss the connection, this quality is repeated in the characters, who seem at times, like Mary Tyrone, to lose their solidity. Laura watches Jim under the light. "JIM: I can't hardly see you sitting way over there. LAURA: I can—see you." (212). "JIM: Look how big my shadow is when I stretch!" (224). "Is my head," Amanda asks, "so transparent?" (180). The image is that of an imaginary creature, so fragile that the slightest accident might make it real, a replica—an imitation of reality, a copy from type, subject to the classifying impulse. "Unicorns—aren't they extinct in the modern world?" (223). "Glass breaks so easily. No matter how careful you are. The traffic jars the shelves and things fall off them" (226). When the unicorn breaks, it is just the replica of a horse. Bereft of its difference, it becomes a reminder, a memory ("a—souvenir" [231]). The fine line between the image and the copy is shattered right before our eyes.

Bentham's inspiration for his Panopticon might have come, Foucault speculates, from Le Vaux's menagerie at Versailles, an indoor, analytical structure very like it, "the first menagerie in which the different elements are not, as they traditionally were, distributed in a park" (Foucault, Discipline 203). "The Panopticon is a royal menagerie; the animal is replaced by man. . . . [T]he Panopticon . . . does the work of a naturalist" (ibid.). "Menagerie," which also means "mixture" (Foucault's synonym for the plague), comes from "ménage," the word for household and household management. Etymologically, then, it suggests less the presence of animals than the logic of human spatial arrangement, a logic that covers its threat of mixture and contamination. But classifying and organizing—however enlightened—cannot produce a stable referent for the infinitely small, ephemeral, and translucent—for what, according to Aristotle, simply cannot be *seen*. The epigraph for *The Glass Menagerie* is from cummings: "Nobody, not even the rain, has such small hands."

Undoubtedly there are dangers in any attempt to remain outside the system of classification, the normal, the true. But classification is after all a kind of confinement, so that protection and exposure amount to the same thing. Laura Wingfield, whose name associates idealistic literary and pictorial art with the image of a bird, gravitates for shelter in the winter toward "the art museum and the bird houses at the Zoo. I visited the penguins every day! . . . Lately I've been spending most of my afternoons in the Jewel Box, that big glass house where they raise the tropical flowers" (155). The enclosure, the classification of art and endangered species, which seems to protect them from "the traffic," also confines them and treats them as commodities of privilege. (Penguins, of course, cannot fly.) Foucault describes the partitioning of the leper as a source of ongoing "dualistic mechanisms of exclusion": "mad/sane; dangerous/harmless; normal/abnormal" in the penitentiary, the school, the hospital, the asylum (Foucault, *Discipline* 199). Zoo and art gallery share an exclusionary function, separating the innocent and the dangerous, the strange and the normal, the fixed and the free from one another, classifying both observer and observed. Underneath the order of analytical space lies the disorder of uncontrollable strangeness. The very word "zoo" is synonymous with chaos. A *glass* menagerie is more vulnerable still.

The spatial obsessions of realism close off territories, dissect them, analyze them, inhabit them with observable types, and erase the means of perceptual control. Williams's play seems to want to explore a discontinuous space, a light, mobile perspective, against the grain of mimetic illusion. And by this spatial technique he gives up a certain power. Ironically freedom of motion seems to mean a loss of territorial rights; Tom's wandering, he says at the end of the play, is a way of "attempting to find in motion what was lost in space" (237). His gradual defection, and civil and world war are in the air from the opening lines. In *The Glass Menagerie*, the power to divide and conquer space is precisely the power that threatens the play with annihilation—"For nowadays the world is lit by lightning! Blow out your candles, Laura." When Laura blows out the candles, the image of the play extinguishes itself, relinquishing its power like some Prospero abandoning a new world. In this play Williams avoids representation's violent implications; he treats them gently, delicately. Glass breaks so easily, and disappointment is not death. No Atlanta burns.[6]

5 A Streetcar Named Desire
Spacial Violation and Sexual Violence

> We see from the *outside* what could not be seen *within.*
> —Tennessee Williams on *Streetcar*

In *A Streetcar Named Desire,* Williams confronts directly the violence implicit in *The Glass Menagerie.* Once again he experiments with space, but in *Streetcar* he examines meaning in its relation to *desire,* that structure of inside and outside, of image and object, that produces the subject. The relation of inside to outside—essence to appearance—is one of representation's great disputes. It is also, more or less, the relation of expressionism to realism. Expressionism's optical distortions, its emphasis on childhood, madness, crime—on emotion as truth's medium—break the connections set up to be analyzed in realism. Realism depends on a stable space and a stable perspective, as we have seen, that enable its mimetic exertions to seem effortless, "natural." What makes the play go is inferred from its surfaces: the past from the present, the inner life from the character, the inner rooms from the visible spaces. The critic's analytical talent is given plenty to work on in this inductive, part-for-the-whole structure. But like cinema, and far more deliberately, expressionism imploded realism's composition, blowing up the inner life until its outer frames snapped. While the principal distinction of "inner-outer," which underlies both dramatic forms, remained firmly in place theoretically, expressionism ended up undermining it in practice. After all, it was an unstable mixture of impression and expression, for how could we have a "pure" expressionist play? How would we be able to *see* it?[1]

The vestiges of realistic space are theoretically behind expressionism, or before it, rather, acting as the reference for "inner" life, providing the objective language for it. Criticism and analysis can never only look at one thing: the comparison implied by mimetic practice is simply reproduced at another level of abstraction. To see something we have always to be looking *past* something else, as realism teaches us to look past a curtain, then past the fourth wall, "into" the scene (chapter 4). Yet this desire to see beyond, as well as into, surfaces is somewhat of the truth this gaze is searching for. It's not an object but a propulsion with a theoretically endless trajectory that won't stop to be analyzed, nor to respect boundaries, but pushes on blindly far out—and in—to space.

Realism is the drama of sexual life: its representation of social and family surfaces via the voyeurism of the fourth wall is designed to get at the hidden behavior of the individual psyche, what people think but don't say, what they do "in private." The omnivorous discourse of realism subsumes every desire into a promised fullness bent on keeping the unspeakable under moral control. But the moral code is elaborated in language, language that proliferates the more it reaches for power. The moral imperative of desire is this: that "you will seek to transform your desire, your every desire, into discourse" (Foucault, *History* 21). As discourse, desire becomes an inexhaustible fountain of metaphor. Realism's repression and secrecy, far from silencing sexual desire, incite a discourse of sexuality. "What is peculiar to modern societies, in fact [Foucault writes], is not that they consigned sex to a shadow existence, but that they dedicated themselves to speaking of it *ad infinitum*, while exploiting it as *the* secret" (Foucault, *History* 35, italics Foucault's). And this is a difficult plot to escape—Foucault has to spend lots of time talking about what he *isn't* talking about. The strategy of inexhaustible revelation is fixity—realism sets representational limits so as to assure truth the bright light of scrutiny.

Meanwhile realism's analytical structure assures the sexual act its pastness, its remoteness: its always-already is reassuringly repetitious, in a code that, promising sex its full revelation, nevertheless prohibits its return. If realism is *the* bourgeois dramatic form, then sex is *the* bourgeois dramatic subject. What can be more crucial than the survival and enrichment of the species, the harnessing of energies for production, the containment of the threat of disorder? Incest, homosexuality, and other "perversions" are completely off the track of realism's linear, evolutionary development, as surely as eugenics, adaptation, and heterosexuality provide its strategic security. "Through the themes of health, progeny, race, the future of the species, the vitality of the social body, power spoke of sexuality and to sexuality" (Foucault, *History* 147). Yet as the word "desire" implies, sexuality has an ambiguous power in language; it is both empirical "truth" and symbolic "representation"—it is "sex" but also more than sex, for sex is "able to function as a unique signifier and as a universal signified" (Foucault, *History* 154). Desire is both bodily sexuality and its "spiritual" tendency, an all-inclusive guide to the smallest points of connection between the hidden and the visible.

> Discourse, therefore, had to trace the meeting line of the body
> and the soul, following all its meanderings: beneath the surface
> of the sins, it would lay bare the unbroken nervure of the
> flesh. Under the authority of a language that had been carefully
> expurgated so that it was no longer directly named, sex was
> taken charge of, tracked down as it were, by a discourse that
> aimed to allow it no obscurity, no respite. [Foucault, *History* 20]

Realism has its roots in the confessional. At the intersection of the (hidden) soul and the (visible) body, a discourse of desire weaves back and forth between flesh and its inner truth, in a language whose subject is "no longer directly named." The language of materiality and the language of ideas are the same.[2] "They told me to take a street-car named Desire, and then transfer to one called Cemeteries and ride six blocks and get off at—Elysian Fields!" (246).

Language's metaphor of experience, spun out, is allegory, as it leaves implicit the comparison it is making between life and life's equivalent expression. Unlike simile, or symbol, metaphor and allegory do not try to enter experience but keep their distance, paralleling life, not intersecting it (cf. de Man 191–92). The fact that the "allegorical" language here describes real places, cars, and transfers has the effect of making its doubleness the more apparent. ("[A]ll desires," de Man warns, "fall prey to the duplicities of expression" [12].) Realism's language is the metaphor of experience; allegory, as de Man reminds us, maintains this doubleness, the "desire for a unity toward which . . . thought and poetic strategy strive" (195). The moment in *The Glass Menagerie* when the unicorn is broken suggests a rupture that makes the representation what it is—the excision of what is uncontainable, of what cannot be "measured" or "copied" from pattern (both related meanings of the word "norm"). The scene enacts the severed connection between image and copy, the containment of desire's excess in the recognizable form. What this broken image offers, then, is not a criticism of reality, nor of artistic representation—the arguments for and against mimesis, respectively—but a reflection on the desire for their union, which is never satisfied.[3] The desire for the union of reality and representation is maintained in allegory, which, rather than merely representing "a meaning that it does not itself constitute," establishes the distance "between the representative and the semantic function of language" (de Man 189). The allegorical thus tends to seem inorganic, apart from experience, "purely mechanical, an abstraction whose original meaning is . . . devoid of substance . . . ; it is an immaterial shape" (ibid. 191–92). The "mechanistic" argument against allegory is telling: form and function must seem indigenous, not forced, empirical, not "abstract." Truth is a found unity, not a sophisticated invention of the mind. We cannot be seen to be making our meanings up.

Through allegory the desire for unity with the real loses none of its indefinite yearning. Williams's plays, with their allegorical language, seem to have a tentative, unfinished character. The ending of *A Streetcar Named Desire* compares the cycle of fertility (spring to fall, pregnancy to birth) with the poker players' game of bluff and chance. These rhythms are not resolutions. Williams's plays thus continually reveal the desire for an ending. Memory or recollection, a sense of its pastness, is crucial to representation and, consequently, as we have seen, to realism, which creates order through the temporalizing of events. Realism's analytical structure starts from a proposed shape or vision of totality and then works backward, breaking it down into reformable segments. The "future" toward which it tends is in fact its starting point. Realism represents desire as something with a goal—"eyes on the finish" (Brecht 37), something that looks past a present into a consoling "future," where a sense of the past and a sense of the future amount to the same thing. In *The Glass Menagerie*, for instance, Amanda's optimistic speeches to Laura, apparently rooted in an idyllic past, are echoed by the Gentleman Caller, who raves about the future. We are used to this parallel in Chekhov: one longing looks pretty much like another. Revealed as a repetitious wandering between body and soul, visible and invisible—unrecapturable—desire loses its sense of an object: it is constantly on the move, "a fundamental pattern of being that discards any possibility of satisfaction" (de Man 17).

The metalanguage of desire seems to preclude development, to deny progress. And yet it seems "natural" to read *A Streetcar Named Desire* as an allegorical journey toward Blanche's apocalyptic destruction at the hands of her "executioner," Stanley. The play's violence, its baroque images of decadence and lawlessness, promises its audience the thrilling destruction of the aristocratic southern Poe-esque mothlike neurasthenic female "Blanche" by the apelike brutish male from the American melting pot. The play is full in fact of realism's developmental language of evolution, "degeneration," eugenics. Before deciding that Stanley is merely an "ape," Blanche sees him as an asset: "Oh I guess he's just not the type that goes for jasmine perfume, but maybe he's what we need to mix with our blood now that we've lost Belle Reve" (285). The surprising thing about this play is that the allegorical reading also seems to be the most "realistic" one, the reading that imposes a unity of language and experience to make structural sense of the play, that is, to make its events organic, natural, inevitable. And yet this reading feels false, because allegorical language resists being pinned down by realistic analysis—it's always only half a story.

But it is possible to close the gap between the language and the stage image, between the stage image and its "double" reality, by a double forgetting: first we must forget that realism is literature, and thus already a metaphor, and then we must forget the distance between allegory and realistic "unity." To say that realism's empiricism is indistinguishable from its metaphor is to set *Streetcar* on a course that is one with a moral, natural ordering of events. Stanley is wrong and Blanche is right, the moralists agree. But the hypocrisy of the "priggish" reading is soon revealed in its ambivalence toward Blanche/Stanley: to make a unity of the play, to order events sequentially, requires a reading that finds Blanche's rape inevitable, a condition of the formal structure: she's the erring woman who gets what she "asks" for (her realistic antecedents are clear). For the prigs, this outcome might not be unthinkable, though it might be—what is worse—distasteful. But Williams seems deliberately to be *making* interpretation a problem: he doesn't exclude the prigs' reading; he invites it. What makes *Streetcar* different from *Glass Menagerie*, let alone O'Neill's late plays, is its constant self-betrayal into and out of analytical norms. The realistic setups in this play really feel like setups, a magician's tricks, inviting readings that leave you hanging from your own schematic noose. Analytically, this play is a trap; it's brilliantly confused; yet without following its false leads, there is no way to get anywhere at all. *Streetcar* has a map, but it's changed the street signs, relying on the impulse of desire to take the play past its plots. In a way it's wrong to say Williams doesn't write endings. He writes elaborate *strings* of them.

Williams has given *Streetcar* strong ties to the reassuring rhetoric of realism. Several references to Stanley's career as "A Master Sergeant in the Engineers' Corps" set the action in the "present," immediately after the war. The geographical location, as with *Glass Menagerie*, is specific, the neighborhood life represented with a greater naturalistic fidelity—"Above the music of the 'Blue Piano' the voices of people on the street can be heard overlapping" (243). Lighting and sound effects may give the scene "a kind of lyricism," but this effect seems itself a realistic touch for "The Quarter." Even the interior set, when it appears (after a similar wipe-out of the fourth wall) resembles *Glass Menagerie* in layout and configuration: a ground floor apartment, with two rooms separated by portieres, occupied by three characters, one of them male.

Yet there are also *troubling* "realistic" details, to which the play seems to point. The mise-en-scène seems to be providing too much enclosure to provide for closure: there's no place for anyone to *go*. There is no fire escape, even though in this play someone does yell "Fire! Fire! Fire!" (sc. 9)—in fact, heat and fire and escape are prominent verbal and visual themes. And the flat does not, as it seems to in *Glass Menagerie*, extend to other rooms beyond the wings but ends in a cul-de-sac: a doorway to the bathroom that becomes Blanche's significant place for escape and "privacy." Most disturbing, perhaps, is not the increased sense of confinement but this absence of privacy, of analytical, territorial space. No gentleman caller invited for supper invades this time, but an anarchic wilderness of French Quarter hoi polloi who spill onto the set and into the flat as negligently as the piano music from the bar around the corner.

There doesn't seem to be anywhere to go to evade the intrusiveness and the violence; when the flat erupts, as it does on the poker night, Stanley's tirade sends Stella and Blanche upstairs to Steve and Eunice, the landlords with, of course, an unlimited run of the house ("We own this place so I can let you in" [248]), whose goings-on are equally violent and uncontained. "You know that one upstairs? (more laughter) One time (laughing) the plaster—(laughing) cracked—" (294). The violence isn't an isolated climax but a repetitive pattern of the action, a state of being—it doesn't resolve anything.

> BLANCH: I'm not used to such—
> MITCH: Naw, it's a shame this had to happen when you just got here. But don't take it serious.
> BLANCHE: Violence! Is so—
> MITCH: Set down on the steps and have a cigarette with me.
> [308]

Anxiety and conflict have become permanent and unresolvable, inconclusive. It isn't clear what, if anything, they *mean*. Unlike realistic drama, which produces clashes in order to push the action forward, *Streetcar* refuses its events a clarity of function, an orderliness.

The ordering of events, which constitutes the temporality of realism, is thus no less arbitrary in *Streetcar* than the ordering of *space*: the outside keeps becoming the inside, and vice versa. Williams has done more to relativize space in *Streetcar* than visualize the fourth wall: the outer wall appears and disappears more than a half-dozen times, often in the middle of a "scene," drawing attention to the spatial illusion rather than making its boundaries absolute. The effect on spatial metaphor is that we are not allowed to forget that it is metaphor and consequently capable of infinite extensions and retractions. As we might expect, the struggle over territory between Stanley and Blanche ("Hey, canary bird! Toots! Get OUT of the BATH-ROOM!" [367]), which indeed results in reasserting the male as "King" (371; Stanley is quoting Huey Long) and pushes Blanche off-stage, punished, defeated, is utterly unanalytical and unsubtle. "*She'll go!* Period. P.S. She'll go Tuesday!" (367). While the expressionistic sequence beginning in scene 6 with Blanche's recollection of "The Grey boy" relativizes space and time, evoking Blanche's memories, it also seems to drain her expressive power until when Stanley is about to rape her she mouths the kinds of things Williams used to put on screens: " 'In desperate, desperate circumstances! Help me! Caught in a trap' " (400). She is establishing her emotions like signposts: "Stay back!" "I warn you, don't, I'm in danger!" (401). What had seemed a way into Blanche's character has had the effect of externalizing her feelings so much that they become impersonal. Space doesn't provide an objective mooring for Blanche's psychology; it keeps turning inside out, obliterating the spatial distinctions that had helped to define the realistic character as someone whose inner life drove the action. Now this driving force of emotion replaces the subtlety of expectation, leaving character out in space, dangling. "There isn't time to be—" Blanche explains into the phone (399); faced with a threatening proximity, she phones long distance and forgets to hang up.

The expressionistic techniques of the latter half of the play abstract the individual from the milieu, and emotion begins to dominate the representation of events. In scene 10, where Blanche and Stanley have their most violent and erotic confrontation, the play loses all sense of boundary. The front of the house is already transparent, but now Williams also dissolves the rear wall, so that beyond the scene with Blanche and Stanley we can see what is happening on the next street.

> A prostitute has rolled a drunkard. He pursues her along the walk, overtakes her and there is a struggle. A policeman's whistle breaks it up. The figures disappear.
>
> Some moments later the Negro Woman appears around the corner with a sequined bag which the prostitute had dropped on the walk. She is rooting excitedly through it. [399]

The mise-en-scène exposes more of the realistic world than before, since now we see the outside as well as the inside of the house at once, and yet the effect is one of intense general paranoia: the threat of violence is "real," not "remembered," and it is everywhere. The walls have become "spaces" along which frightening, "sinuous" shadows weave—"lurid," "grotesque and menacing." The parameters of Blanche's presence are unstable images of threatening "flames" of desire, and this sense of sexual danger seems to draw the action toward itself. So it is as though Blanche somehow "suggests" rape to Stanley—it is already in the air; we can see it being given to him as if it were a thought. "You think I'll interfere with you? Ha-ha! . . . Come to think of it—maybe you wouldn't be bad to—interfere with" (401).

The "inner-outer" distinctions of both realistic and expressionistic representation are shown coming together here. Williams makes no effort to suggest that the "lurid" expressionistic images in scene 10 are all in Blanche's mind, as cinematic point of view would: the world outside the house is the realistic world of urban poverty and violence. But it is also the domain of the brutes, whose "inhuman jungle voices rise up" as Stanley, snakelike, tongue between his teeth, closes in. The play seems to swivel on this moment, when the logic of appearance and essence, the individual and the abstract, turns inside out, like the set, seeming to occupy for once the same space. It is either the demolition of realistic objectivity or the transition point at which realism takes over some new territory. At this juncture "objective" vision becomes an "outside" seen from inside; for the abstraction that allows realism to represent truth objectively cannot itself be explained as objectivity. The surface in scene 10 seems to be disclosing, without our having to look too deeply, a static primal moment beneath the immediacy of the action: the sexual taboo underneath realistic discourse.

> BLANCHE: Stay back! Don't you come toward me another step or I'll—
> STANLEY: What?
> BLANCHE: Some awful thing will happen! It will!
> STANLEY: What are you putting on now?
>   (They are now both inside the bedroom.)
> BLANCHE: I warn you, don't, I'm in danger!
> [401]

What "will happen" in the bedroom doesn't have a name or even an agency. The incestuous relation lies beyond the moral and social order of marriage and the family, adaptation and eugenics, not to mention (as Williams reminds us here) the fact that it's unmentionable. Whatever words Blanche uses to describe it scarcely matter. As

Stella says, "I couldn't believe her story and go on living with Stanley" (405).

The rape in *Streetcar* thus seems familiar and inevitable, even to its "characters," who lose the shape of characters and become violent antagonists as if on cue. "Oh! So you want some roughhouse! All right, let's have some roughhouse!" (402). When Blanche sinks to her knees, it's as if the action is an acknowledgment. Stanley holds Blanche, who has become "inert," he carries her to bed. She is not only silent but crumpled, immobile, while he takes over control and agency. He literally places her on the set. But Williams does not suggest that Stanley is conscious and autonomous; on the contrary the scene is constructed so as to make him as unindividuated as Blanche: they seem, at this crucial point, more than ever part of an allegorical landscape. In a way, it's the *impersonality* of the rape that is most telling: the obliteration of individuation and the spatial distinctions that allow for "character." Expressionistically, then, character dissolves into an overwhelming mise-en-scène that produces emotion as a landscape. The rape scene ends without words, without conflict, without characters.

Perhaps *Streetcar*—and Williams—present problems for those interested in Pirandellian metatheater. Metatheater assumes a self-consciousness of dramatic form; but Williams makes the "form" *everything*. It isn't arbitrary, or stifling: Stanley and Blanche are not characters struggling to get out of their "plot." Character is the expression of the form; it is not accidental or originary. Like Brecht, Williams does not see character as a humanist impulse raging against fatal abstractions. (In a play like *The Good Person of Setzuan*, for example, Brecht makes a kind of comedy of this "tragedy.") Plays are not about people. They're about thought and feeling; they represent these things. If this seems to suggest that the rape in *Streetcar* is something other than a rape, and so not a rape, it also suggests that it is as much a rape as it is possible for it to be. While exposing the essence of appearances, as Williams says, seeing from outside what can't be seen from within, the scene exposes its own scenic limitations for dramatizing that which cannot be in the scene: namely, the act it represents.

Both the surface "street scene" and the jungle antecedents of social order are visible, outside and inside, thoroughly violating the norms of realism's analytical space. When Stanley "springs" at Blanche, overturning the table, it is clear that a last barrier has been broken down, and now there is no space that is outside the jungle. "We've had this date with each other from the beginning!" (402). We've regressed to some awful zero point (or hour). "A fetid swamp," one critic said of Williams's plays, by way of description. We are also back at the *heart* of civilization, at its root, the incest taboo, and the center of sexuality, which is oddly enough also the center of realism: the family, where "sexuality is 'incestuous' from the start" (Foucault, *History* 108–109). At the border of civilization and the swamp is the sexual transgression whose suppression is the source of all coercive order. Through allegory, Williams makes explicit what realism obscures, forcing the sexuality that propels discourse into the content of the scene.

The destruction of spatial boundaries visualizes the restless discourse of desire, that uncontainable movement between inside and outside, soul and body. "Desire," Williams writes in his short story "Desire and the Black Masseur," "is something that is made to occupy a larger space than that which is afforded by the individual being" (Williams, *Stories* 217). "Desire" derives from the Latin word for "star" ("Stella for Star!"); an archaic sense is "to feel the loss of": the individual is a sign of incompleteness, not self-sufficiency, whose defining gesture is an indication of the void beyond the visible, not its closure. The consciousness of desire as a void without satisfaction is the rejection of realism's "virtual space," which tries to suggest that its fractured space implied an unseen totality. Realism's objectivity covered up its literariness, as if the play were not created from nothing but evolved out of a reality one had but to look to see. But literature answers the desire for a fullness that remains unfilled—it never intersects reality, never completes a trajectory; it remains in orbit. The nothing from which literature springs, whole, cannot be penetrated by a vision, even a hypothetical one, and no time can be found for its beginning. As de Man reasons in his discussion of Lévi-Strauss's metaphor of "virtual focus," logical sight lines may be imaginary, but they are not "fiction," any more than "fiction" can be explained as logic:

The virtual focus is a quasi-objective structure posited to give rational integrity to a process that exists independently of the self. The subject merely fills in, with the dotted line of geometrical construction, what natural reason had not bothered to make explicit; it has a passive and unproblematic role. The "virtual focus" is, strictly speaking, a nothing, but its nothingness concerns us very little, since a mere act of reason suffices to give it a mode of being that leaves the rational order unchallenged. The same is not true of the imaginary source of fiction. Here the human self has experienced the void within itself and the invented fiction, far from filling the void, asserts itself as pure nothingness, our nothingness stated and restated by a subject that is the agent of its own instability. [19]

Nothingness, then, the impulse of "fiction," is not the result of a supposed originary act of transgression, a mere historical lapse at the origin of history that can be traced or filled in by a language of logic and analysis; on the contrary, fiction is the *liberation* of a pure consciousness of desire as unsatisfied yearning, a space without boundaries.

Yet we come back to Blanche's rape by her brother-in-law, which seems visibly to reseal the laws of constraint, to justify the logic of lost beginnings. Reenacting the traumatic incestuous moment enables history to begin over again, while the suppression of inordinate desire resumes the order of sanity: Stella is silenced; Blanche is incarcerated. And if there is some ambivalence about Blanche's madness and her exclusion, it is subsumed in an argument for order and a "healthy" redirection of desire. In the last stage direction, Stanley's groping fingers discover the opening of Stella's blouse. The final setup feels inevitable; after all, the game is still "Seven-card stud," and aren't we going to have to "go on" by playing it? The play's return to realistic (and we might also say, heterosexual) logic seems assured, and Williams is still renouncing worlds. He points to the closure of the analytical reading with deft disingenuousness. Closure was always just next door to entrapment; Williams seems to be erasing their boundary lines.

Madness, the brand of exclusion, objectifies Blanche and enables her to be analyzed and confined as the embodiment of nonbeing, an expression of something beyond us and so structured in language (Foucault, *Madness* 100). "There isn't a goddam thing but imagination! . . . And lies and conceit and tricks!" Stanley says (398). The containment of desire's excess through the exclusion of madness creates, as Foucault has argued, a conscience on the perimeters of society, setting up a boundary between inside and outside ("[The madman] is put in the interior of the exterior, and inversely"; Foucault, *Madness* 11). Blanche is allegorically a reminder that liberty can also be captivity, just as her libertinage coincides with her desire for death (her satin robe is a passionate red, she calls Stanley her "executioner," etc.). And Blanche senses early on the threat of confinement; she keeps trying (perversely) to end the play. "I have to plan for us both, to get us both—out!" she tells Stella, after the fight with Stanley that seems, to Blanche, so final (320).

But in the end the play itself seems to have some trouble letting go of Blanche. Having created its moving boundary line, it no longer knows where to put her; what "space" does her "madness" occupy? As the dialogue suggests, she has to go—somewhere; she has become excessive. Yet she keeps coming back: "I'm not quite ready." "Yes! Yes, I forgot something!" (412, 414). Again she is chased around the bedroom, this time by the Matron, while "The 'Varsouviana' is filtered into a weird distortion, accompanied by the cries and noises of the jungle," the "lurid," "sinuous" reflections on the walls (414). The Matron's lines are echoed by other "mysterious voices" somewhere beyond the scene; she sounds "like a firebell." "Matron" and "Doctor" enter the play expressionistically, as functional agents, and Blanche's paranoia is now hers alone: the street is not visible. The walls don't disintegrate; they come alive. Blanche is inside her own madness, self-imprisoned: her madness is precisely her enclosure within the image (cf. Foucault, *Madness* 94). In her paranoid state, Blanche really cannot "get out," because there isn't any longer an outside: madness transgresses and transforms boundaries, "forming an act of undetermined content" (ibid. 94). It thus negates the image while remaining imprisoned within it; the boundaries of the scene are not helping to define Blanche but reflecting her back to herself.

Blanche's power is not easy to suppress; she is a reminder that beneath the appearance of order something nameless has been lost.

"What's happened here? I want an explanation of what's happened here," she says "with sudden hysteria" (408, 407). It is a reasonable request that cannot be reasonably answered. This is the same problem posed at the end of *The Glass Menagerie*: how to escape from the image when it seems to have been given too much control, when its reason is absolute? Expressionism threatens the reason of realistic mise-en-scène by taking it perhaps too far, stretching the imagination beyond limits toward an absoluteness of the image, a desire of desire. The "mimetic" mirror now becomes the symbol of madness; the image no longer simply reflects desire (desire of, desire for) but subsumes the mirror itself into the language of desire. When Blanche shatters her mirror (391), she (like Richard II) shows that her identity has already been fractured; she doesn't see herself in the mirror; she sees the mirror as herself. And she cries out when the lantern is torn off the lightbulb, because there is no longer a space between the violence she experiences and the image of that violence. The inner and the outer worlds fuse; the reflecting power of the image is destroyed as it becomes fully *self*-reflective. The passion of madness exists somewhere in between determinism and expression, which at this point "actually form only one and the same movement which cannot be dissociated except after the fact" (Foucault, *Madness* 88).

But realism, that omnivorous discourse, can subsume even the loss of the subjective-objective distinction—when determinism equals expression—and return to some quasi-objective perspective. Thus at the very moment when all space seems to have been conquered, filled in and opened up, there is a need to parcel it out again into clearly distinguishable territories. Analysis normalizes desire. At the end of *A Streetcar Named Desire*, there is a little drama. Blanche's wild expressionistic images are patronized and pacified by theatricality: "I—just told her that—we'd made arrangements for her to rest in the country. She's got it mixed up in her mind with Shep Huntleigh" (404–405). Her family plays along with Blanche's delusions, even to costuming her in her turquoise seahorse pin and her artificial violets. The Matron tries to subdue her with physical violence, but Blanche is only really overcome by the Doctor's politeness.

Formerly an expressionistic "type," having "the unmistakable aura of the state institution with its cynical detachment" (411), the Doctor "takes off his hat and now he becomes personalized. The unhuman quality goes. His voice is gentle and reassuring as he crosses to Blanche and crouches in front of her. As he speaks her name, her terror subsides a little. The lurid reflections fade from the walls, the inhuman cries and noises die out and her own hoarse crying is calmed" (417). Blanche's expressionistic fit is contained by the Doctor's realistic transformation: he is particularized; he can play the role of gentleman caller. Straitjacket, Doctor? the Matron asks him. He smiles. It won't be necessary (417–18). As they exit, Blanche's visionary excesses have clearly been surrendered to him; "She allows him to lead her as if she were blind" (418). Stylistically, here, realism replaces expressionism at the exact moment when expressionism's "pure subjectivity" seems ready to annihilate the subject, to result in her violent subjugation. At this point the intersubjective dialogue returns, clearly masking—indeed, blinding—the subjective disorder with a reassuring form. If madness is perceived as a kind of "social failure" (Foucault, *Madness* 259), social success is to be its antidote.

Of course theater is a cure for madness: by dramatizing or literalizing the image one destroys it. Such theatricality might risk its own confinement in the image, and for an instant there may be a real struggle in the drama between the image and the effort to contain it. Using illusion to destroy illusion requires a forgetting of illusion, of the representational break illusion has to deny. "The artificial reconstitution of delirium constitutes the real distance in which the sufferer recovers his liberty" (ibid. 190). In fact there is no return to "intersubjectivity," just a kind of formal recognition of it: "Whoever you are—I have always depended on the kindness of strangers" (418). *Streetcar* makes the return to normality gentle and theatrical, while "revealing" much more explicitly than *The Glass Menagerie* the violence that is thereby suppressed. This violence isn't "reality" but yet another theater underneath the theater of ruse; the cure of illusion ironically is "effected by the suppression of theater" (Foucault, *Madness* 191).[4]

The realistic containment at the end of *Streetcar* thus does not quite make it back all the way to realism's objective "historical" truth. History, structured by relations of power, not relations to meaning (Foucault, *Power/Knowledge* 114), sometimes assumes the power of reality itself, the platonic Form behind realism, so to speak. When it becomes the language of authority, history also assumes the authority of language, rather naively trusting language to be the reality it represents. The bloody wars and strategic battles are soon forgotten into language, the past tense, the fait accompli. History is the waste of time and the corresponding conquest of space, and realism is the already conquered territory, the belated time with the unmistakable stamp of authenticity. It gets applause simply by being plausible; it forgets that it is literature. To read literature, as de Man says, we ought to remember what we have learned from it—that the expression and the expressed can never entirely coincide, that no single observation point is trustworthy (11). *Streetcar*'s powerful explosion of allegorical language and expressionistic images keeps its vantage point on the move, at a remove. Every plot is untied. Realism rewards analysis, and Williams invites it, perversely, but any analysis results in dissection; to provide *Streetcar* with an exegesis seems like gratuitous destruction, "deliberate cruelty." Perhaps no other U.S. writer since Dickinson has seemed so easy to crush.

And this consideration ought to give the writer who has defined Blanche's "madness" some pause. Even the critical awareness of her tidy incarceration makes for too tidy a criticism. In Derrida's analysis of Foucault's *Madness and Civilization*, he questions the possibility of "historicizing" something that doesn't exist outside of the imprisonment of history, of speech—madness "simply says the other of each determined form of the logos" (Derrida, *Writing* 58). Madness, Derrida proposes, is a "hyperbole" out of which "finite-thought, that is to say, history" establishes its "reign," by the "disguised internment, humiliation, fettering and mockery of the madman within us, of the madman who can only be the fool of a logos which is father, master and king" (60–61). Philosophy arises from the "*confessed* terror of going mad" (62); it is the "economic" embrace of madness (61–62).

To me, then, Williams's play seems to end quite reasonably with a struggle, at the point in the play in which structure and coherence must assert themselves (by seeming to)—that is, the end of the play. The end must look back, regress, so as to sum up and define. It has no other choice. The theatrical ending always becomes, in fact, the real ending. It cannot remain metaphorically an "end." And what is visible at the end is Blanche in trouble, trapped, mad. She is acting as though she believed in a set of events—Shep Huntleigh's rescue of her—that the other characters, by their very encouragement, show to be unreal. There is a fine but perhaps important distinction here: Blanche's acting is no more convincing than theirs, but, and Derrida makes this point about madness, she is thinking things before they can be historicized, that is, before they have happened or even have been shown to be likely or possible (reasonable). "Is not what is called finitude possibility as crisis?" Derrida asks (62). The other characters, who behave as if what Blanche is saying were real, underline her absurdity precisely by invoking reality.

Blanche's relation to history and to structural authority are laid bare by this "forced" ending, in which she repeatedly questions the meaning of meaning: "What has happened here?" The question implies the relativity of space and moment and so of "events" and their meanings, which are at this point impossible to separate. For this reason it's important that the rape suggest an overthrow of meaning, not only through a stylized emphasis on its own representation but also through its strongly relativized temporality. (Blanche warns against what "will happen" while Stanley says the event is the future, the fulfillment of a "date" or culmination in time promised "from the beginning.")

Indeed, the problem of madness lies precisely in this gap between past and future, as we have seen in chapters 2 and 3, in the structural slippage between the temporal and the ontological. For if madness, as Derrida suggests, can exist at all outside of opposition (to reason), it must exist in "hyperbole," in the excess prior to its incarceration in structure, meaning, time, and coherence. A truly "mad" person would not objectify madness—would not, that is, define and locate it. For that reason all discussions of "madness" tend to essentialize it, by insisting, like Blanche's fellow characters at the end of Streetcar, that it is real, that it exists. And the final stroke of logic, the final absurdity, is that, in order to insist that madness exists, to objectify and to define and to relate to it, it is necessary to deny it any history. Of course "madness" is not at all amenable to history, to structure, causality, rationality, recognizable "thought." But this denial of the history of madness has to come from within history itself, from within the language of structure and "meaning." Blanche's demand to know "what has happened here"—her insistence that something "has happened," however one takes it—has to be unanswerable. It can't go any further. In theatrical terms, the "belief" that would make that adventure of meaning possible has to be denied, shut down. But this theatrical release isn't purifying; on the contrary, it's gotten up close to the plague, to the point at which reason and belief contaminate each other: the possibility of thinking madly. Reason and madness can cohabit with nothing but a thin curtain between. And curtains aren't walls; they don't provide solid protection.[5]

Submitting Williams's allegorical language to realistic analysis, then, leads to conclusions: the imprisonment of madness, the redirection of desire. The moral meaning smoothes things over. Planning to "open up" Streetcar for the film version with outside scenes and flashbacks, Elia Kazan found it wouldn't work—he ended up making the walls movable so they could actually close in more with every scene (Kazan 384). Williams's dramatic language is too free, too wanton; it's a trap, it's asking to be analyzed, it lies down on the couch. Kazan saw this perverse desire in the play—he thought Streetcar was about Williams's cruising for tough customers: "The reference to the kind of life Tennessee was leading at the time was clear. Williams was aware of the dangers he was inviting when he cruised; he knew that sooner or later he'd be beaten up. And he was" (351).

But Kazan undervalues the risk Williams is willing to take. It isn't just violence that cruising invites; it's death. And that desire, as O'Neill found in the end of Iceman, can't be realized. Since there's really no way to get what you want, you have to put yourself in a position where you don't always want what you get. In pursuing desire beyond "reason"—psychoanalytic, theatrical, or otherwise—Williams exposes the violence of representation. The complicitousness of art and violence (or submission to violence) is not lost on him, as he makes clear in the end of "Desire and the Black Masseur." Anthony Burns is cannibalized by the masseur, who has already beaten him to pulp, and thus, consumed by his desire, Burns makes up for what Williams calls his "incompletion." For violence, like art, masks the incompletion, the inadequacy, the hole or gap, through which desire, like representation, seeks closure. "Yes, it is perfect," thinks the masseur, whose manipulations have tortured Burns to death. "It is now completed!"

Afterword

"To begin with, I turn back time." Here I want to make a contradictory move similar to Tom Wingfield's in *The Glass Menagerie*: to end by looking forward to the playwrights whom O'Neill and Williams anticipate and so to ask where left-wing U.S. drama has gone since the crisis of the thirties and forties.

The turning point of representation I've described here points U.S. drama in the direction of poststructuralist theory's concerns with time, materiality, representation, the uses of history, and the possibility of political efficacy. O'Neill and Williams's plays extend and explore classic modernist themes, such as the breakdown of reliable structures of meaning and the desire for a national narrative. Yet these themes are extended outward in their plays, away from the individual, the perspectival, and toward a radical questioning of representation. In the plays I have been discussing, there is no point of view that anchors experience/time/meaning, no totalizing philosophy to replace what has been lost. Instead, these plays explore multiple sites of interpretation and end indefinitely, with no way of looking back from a summary position. Social realism as a kind of literalism is thereby abandoned, and its potential for redeployment liberated. Williams and O'Neill have the same insight into realism, namely, that its mimetic assumptions have tended to close off possibilities for social criticism that lie precisely in the fantastic. Williams's flights of fantasy are never reducible to the individual unconscious, say, or to any other conventional "expressionistic" alienation from the real. On the contrary, he puts the real/fantastic in suspense, bringing it continually to question. Williams's approach shares with poststructuralism its positive rethinking of the relation between reality and representation as the very sources of writing and dramatic innovation.

Central to this book is the notion that progressive or left-wing drama in the United States since World War II has tended away from social realism without simply rejecting it. The concerns with materialism and social change turn to the problem of change *from* what *to* what, questioning the desire for an object, indeed, making something named "desire" the focus of the drama. Postwar philosophy has inquired after the difficulty, if not the impossibility, of measuring change. If time, linearity, history, even "difference" are inseparable from their constructions in time, space, and "culture"—that is, inseparable from their enunciations in specific contexts—then what "past" are we changing from, exactly? And what does "the future" mean? How is it possible to think or to act in the present? These are the questions this book takes up in O'Neill's and Williams's plays that have helped to define poststructuralism's reaction to modernism's lost meanings and its saving structures. These plays suggest an idea of history as a construction that is nonetheless real and powerful, with the result that fantasy no longer competes with the real on the U.S. stage.

In the sixties and seventies, however, Williams's new work was scarcely read or acted. Edward Albee, Lanford Wilson, and Sam Shepard, in their different ways, continued the development of a theater of language and the exploration of an explicitly reconstructed "past." *Who's Afraid of Virginia Woolf?* (1962), *The Rimers of Eldritch* (1966), and *The Tooth of Crime* (1972), for example, all question time, history, sexuality, and U.S. cultural "values." Lanford Wilson in particular found his métier in the continuing U.S. obsession with revaluing history. Meanwhile, Adrienne Kennedy, a black woman writer, was producing avant-garde one-act plays that were far more daringly fantastic than the work of these more celebrated male playwrights. Inspired in part by the new black theater and in part by Williams's plays, and encouraged by Albee, Kennedy produced a style that deployed cultural "influences" as icons, projections, and distorting mirrors. An influence and a history imply a subject influenced and historicized, but Kennedy's work shows, as Foucault's has, how much that "subject" is an effect of these cultural forces, and not their preexisting condition. Kennedy brought to the traditional modern themes of loss, family, history, and the individual the culturally relative notions of race, gender, and identity.

Kennedy's early plays combine quiet, graceful, even lyrical writing with violent imagery, both verbal and visual. But with *A Movie Star Has to Star in Black and White* (1976), by now her best-known play, Kennedy seemed to be looking back over her own work of the sixties, changing her tone, and producing fantasy images that were more textured and less spectacular. *Movie Star* in fact seems to look back to Williams and specifically to *The Glass Menagerie*, the play Kennedy says first made her think of writing drama. Kennedy had originally found Williams too realistic; she says she had to force herself to stop trying to imitate him. But in *Movie Star*, *The Glass Menagerie* finally reappears in Kennedy's work as a very faint underlayer in a palimpsest that superimposes layer after layer of narrative, including the narrative of Kennedy's own composition of her early plays. As the idea of the palimpsest suggests, in this play, writing's materialization is inseparable from its temporal and spatial relations. Kennedy's obsession with transformable rooms and spaces in earlier plays such as *Funnyhouse of a Negro* and *The Owl Answers* leads her in *Movie Star* to even more multiple, noncentered, mobile crossings. In this play all the narratives color each other, so that even "tragic" stories, like the one about her brother's car accident and paralysis, are productive, suggestive, and moving—not paralyzed.

Movie Star seems to echo both *Long Day's Journey into Night* and *The Glass Menagerie*, as a black woman who wants to write narrates the story of her family: her parents' estrangement and her brother's alienation. Like those earlier plays, Kennedy's play turns back the clock. *Movie Star* keeps returning to the image of the silent brother, who, paralyzed and comatose, lies in a hospital bed, present yet absent, a focal point for the family narrative that swirls around him. The narrator, Clara, is trying to write a new play, and she records her memories and impressions as we watch. In *Movie Star* the crisis of representation entwines intricately with the crises of identity and action. Clara is not the "star" of the story or of the play; she plays "a bit role," watching passively while the scenes of her life are performed by white movie-star lookalikes on the sets of their famous movies of the forties and fifties. Like Williams's *Menagerie*, *Movie Star* invokes film technique, with its superimpositions, highlighting, and fadeouts, building into the very structure of the play *Menagerie*'s suggestion that film "fantasy" and "real" life were coming closer together. The final lines describe Clara holding her mother, feeling that they might both fall headlong down a flight of stairs. It's an image of imbalance, of suspense; like Williams's endings, it's understated and unresolved.

Of her parents, Clara/Bette Davis says, "The only reality I wanted never came true . . . to be their angel of mercy to unite them" (*In One Act* 83). In Tony Kushner's *Angels in America* (1992–1993), an angel does finally arrive, though she's not much of a mercy. Like Kennedy and Williams, Kushner writes fantastically with one foot in the real, combining huge emotional and political stakes with a nonjudgmental, antisentimental approach. Kennedy's fantasies of assimilation explore the contradiction between the constructed identity and the "self" who would "construct" it through assimilation; Kushner's play begins by defining assimilation as a national fiction, "the melting-pot where nothing melted" (*Millennium* 10). Kennedy suggests identity as textured, layered, elusive; Kushner explicitly rejects "Individualism" and "the political economy it serves, capitalism" ("Afterword" in *Perestroika* 152), citing Brecht, who once observed that the word "individual" is a misnomer if ever there was one. Kushner's play is full of crises, collisions, split scenes, crashes, broken plaster; it's entirely composed of breakdowns or what I've called in Williams elaborate strings of endings. Breakdowns aren't endings, as Kushner sees, they're productive. In his play opposites aren't absorbed or assimilated but go on dialectically, relentlessly. *Perestroika* opens with the aged Bolshevik asking whether and how change is possible and ends with the conviction that change is inevitable. Kushner's concern is whether we look at change with self-protectiveness, fear, and loathing or with coalition, energy, and love.

Kushner finds his dramatic opportunity in the escalating confusion of representation and politics in the Reagan eighties, when progressiveness was equated with conservatism, and idealism with materialism. Roy Cohn is the most audacious example of Kushner's deconstruction of these oppositions; he's a neoconservative conservative whose visions of power and insiderness are messily crossed by their apparent antitheses: Ethel Rosenberg, homosexuality, and AIDS. Kushner writes Cohn a great part, yet Cohn's ties to the history of U.S. politics are written into the play as well, and Kushner is careful to underscore them in the production notes. Like the angelic visitation in Kushner's play, so reminiscent of Williams's and Kennedy's fascination with winged things, Cohn materializes fantastically. And in this way Kushner demonstrates the contradiction of social action in the United States at the end of the twentieth century: "We live past hope" (*Perestroika* 136).

Notes

1. INTRODUCTION: EUGENE O'NEILL, TENNESSEE WILLIAMS, AND U.S. DRAMATIC THEORY, 1935–1947

1. To get a sense of Plato's use of the word "mimesis" in both broad and limited ways, see *The Republic* books 3 and 10. For an overview of its appropriation since then, see Spariosu, "Editor's Introduction" (I–XXIX).

2. Cf. *The Republic*, 605c: " '[T]he dramatic poet produces similarly a bad state of affairs in the mind of the individual, by encouraging the unreasoning part of it, . . . and by creating images far removed from the truth.' " (I rely throughout this chapter, as elsewhere in the book, on the Penguin Classics editions of Plato and Aristotle. The page numbers and section letters are the standard references, given whenever these are provided by the Penguin translator.)

3. On the meanings of "pleasure," see, e.g.: Plato, *The Republic* 390a, 397d–98b, 505bff., and 607bff.; *The Laws* 667–69; and Aristotle, *The Politics* 1337b33–38a13, and 1339b10–39b31.

4. T. J. Saunders, translator of *The Laws* for the Penguin Classics series, notes that "the translator of *The Laws* is plagued to an unusual degree" by the text's "elephantine punning and other kinds of word-play, usually impossible to reproduce in English," and by its "difficult" use of the Greek, "emphatic yet imprecise, elaborate yet careless, prolix yet curiously elliptical; the meaning is often obscure and the translator is forced to turn interpretor" (39). Besides reminding the reader that any "reading" of Plato, including my own, is interpretive and positional, I quote these lines to reinforce my sense that Plato is deeply aware of the irony of writing—aware, that is, of his own role as interpreter and artist.

5. Wilde, like Plato, retains the notion of a mimetic correspondence between art and reality, which is why his inversions of logic are shaped like logic—in epigrams.

6. For analyses of Aristotle's notion of the uses of pleasure, and of learning through imitation, see Spariosu IX and Nussbaum 342.

7. Aristotle discusses the relevance of intent and of an action's conditions—and hence of the viewpoint of the one who acts—in *On the Art of Poetry* 71 and 73.

8. Timothy J. Wiles discusses Brecht's debt to Aristotle in chap. 3.

9. The behavioral and anthropological approach to play, as something observed, a way of ordering and performing culture, thus a part of what is readable from culture to culture, has been very persuasively worked out in performance theory, especially by Victor Turner. See, e.g., his book *From Ritual to Theatre*. In *The Anthropology of Performance*, Turner extended the notion of play to the cognitive function, the limbic system of the brain. The empiricism of much performance theory already assumes—and underscores—much of what I have to say about the social and political uses of the art/life distinction. In fact performance theory demonstrates an implicit mimetic concern in its sense of "play" as something ritual, lived, and "performed" rather than simply repeated or imitated. Herbert Blau has pointed out the necessary *system* surrounding "play" in *The Eye of Prey*, chap. 8.

10. See Diamond. Although I suppose, as Spariosu seems to be saying, we might *imagine* a mimesis outside the power relations inherent in referential language—indeed Derrida has suggested that such a capacity for imagination is the very thing that makes philosophical thought possible (*Writing and Difference* 61)—I think Foucault's demonstration of the deeply intricate links between putative "sources" and "effects" of power ought to make us chary of how we express these imaginings. Derrida engages with Plato in many of his texts. For his overview of Plato's notion of mimesis, see *Dissemination* 186–87, n.14; and for a discussion of Platonic "play," see *Dissemination* 156–58.

11. In recent years there has been new work on the question of audience. See, e.g., Susan Bennett; Herbert Blau, *The Audience*; and Daphna Ben Chaim, *Distance in the Theatre*.

12. This of course is not to say that all art is in some simple way, and of necessity, politically polemical, environmentally determined, etc., but rather that art cannot escape the conditions under which it becomes art: like language, it is captured as soon as it is set free.

13. Cf. Herbert Lindenberger; and Hanna Scolnikov 91, 96.

14. For Derrida's witty exploration of the borders between sending and receiving, and Plato's correspondence to Socrates, see *The Post Card*.

15. In fact it has been quite common for historians of the thirties to downplay the political content of the drama of the period, and refer to left-

wing plays as "moral" or "reformist." See, e.g., Harold Clurman, *The Fervent Years,* as well as his introduction to *Famous American Plays of the 1930's;* and Himelstein.

16. Ironically, the revolutionary will of the hero was thus, in effect, demanded as artistic policy. The socialist concern with audience as participant was accompanied by the oppression of artists for their subject matter (see below). In the 1940s and after, the period of the "Zhdanovschina," Soviet policy took this exclusionary theory to its literal and murderous conclusion. In Stalin's Soviet Union (as in the United States today), the arts and not the sciences became the scene of ideological strategy. See, e.g., Gavriel D. Ra'anan, chaps. 4 and 5; and for another view, Werner G. Hahn.

17. For a positive assessment of these liberal-humanist elements of Aristotle's theory of art, see Nussbaum.

18. For varying accounts of the events of the late 1930s and their effects on U.S. theater, see, e.g., Himelstein; Hallie Flanagan; Jane De Hart Mathers; Ira A. Levine; and Jay Williams.

19. Mihai Spariosu includes in his list of French theorists who have influenced the current debate on mimesis Barthes, Derrida, Girard, and Genette (I).

20. As Joel Black notes in "Idolology: The Model in Artistic Practice and Critical Theory" (in Spariosu 172–200), the challenge to "the long-standing mimetic concept of art" (173) has been dominated by French theorists such as Foucault, Genette, Riffaterre, Derrida, and Girard (196 n.5).

21. On the power of mimesis as a way of perceiving as well as producing art, see, e.g., Lindenberger; Erich Auerbach; and E. H. Gombrich.

22. "The twentieth-century stage still adheres to a nineteenth-century style that it continues to recognize as old-fashioned and dated but which it cannot discard for lack of anything to put in its place" (Gassner 14). The persistence of mimetic issues in criticism has been restated as recently as 1989 by Hanna Scolnikov, e.g.: "Aristotelian mimesis continues to haunt the critical scene, demanding to be reckoned with, refusing to be disregarded" (91).

23. Performance theory, certainly, urges us beyond the visible, supposing, at times, the act of seeing to create performance wherever it looks, opening up the world as our theater in its inclusiveness. This notion of performance theory is noticeable in Richard Schechner. Compare Herbert Blau's assessment of performance in *The Eye of Prey,* where he questions such "Universals of Performance" (chap. 8). For Schechner, I suggest, performance theory redefines the mimetic question by seeing performance as a

universal human condition from which drama and the theater spring, traceable to hunting or agriculture (much as Victor Turner found it traceable to the brain's limbic system). As performance theorists demonstrate, the demarcation of "art" and "life" is not as clear in cultures not influenced by Western philosophy. My project in this book is precisely to discuss where I see Western philosophy's influence on modern dramatic theory, especially in the United States.

24. Realism's persistence into the twentieth century was anticipated in the nineteenth, when it was closely tied to social reform and scientific experimentation and so managed continually to redefine itself as reflective of the real, in the evolving (and evolutionary) sense of that term. This tendency is visible from Zola's naturalism to Ibsen's psychospiritual "realism," Shaw's "realistic" abandoning of ethical systems ("A Dramatic Realist to His Critics"), and on to Lukács and Emma Goldman in the twentieth century. In *The Idea of a Theater*, Francis Fergusson attempted to explain this durability by showing that modern realism really returns to Aristotelian "movement of the psyche" (148).

25. *Long Day's Journey into Night*, for example, seems to have been conceived as a book rather than something to be performed, as a letter to Bennett Cerf at Random House in 1951 stipulates: "No, I do not want [to be sent a copy of] *Long Day's Journey Into Night*. That, as you know, is to be published twenty-five years after my death—but never produced as a play" (Letter 559, June 13, 1951, p. 589). Kurt Eisen has described O'Neill's style as a fusion of melodrama and the modern novel.

26. *The Iceman Cometh* is often compared to *The Wild Duck*, since both plays seem critical of truth telling. The alternative, presumably, is "illusion," which is to say, "art"—so goes the conventional wisdom. The mimetic-realistic issue of representation increases the complexity—indeed the self-reflexivity—of such a claim (and of such analogy), for in mimesis the truth-illusion problem is not at all the problem of mutually exclusive terms, much less values. On the contrary, it is the conundrum of all representational art that lays (as it must) claims to any kind of truth. Thus Ibsen and O'Neill's plays seem to contradict the very assumption underlying the notion that their plays argue *against* truth and *for* illusion. I might say these plays complicate the notion that you can ever tell the truth *at all*, or that, in mimetic terms, the representation of anything is ever the truth of it.

27. I have already mentioned Plato's theorizing about space in relation to his Form/Copy theory (in *Timaeus* 71–72). Here it is also relevant that the word "genesis" ("change") as Plato uses it refers to physical and visual

objects and hence to the realm of mutability—that is, the realm of representation. (See *The Republic* 345 n.) For Plato, then, representation binds the possibility of perception to an external world that changes over time.

28. That O'Neill and Williams can be described as "left-wing" writers, however, is not really in dispute. An FBI file existed on O'Neill quite early in his career, and Williams's early work seems to have included agit-prop drama. See, e.g., Bruce J. Mann, "An FBI Memorandum on O'Neill."

29. David Savran has argued for Williams's relevance to postmodernism, if not poststructuralism. Only recently, Savran writes, has it become possible "to understand not just Williams's deep antipathy to theatrical realism, but also his status as a postmodernist *avant la lettre*" (98). For further reflections on Williams from a postmodern perspective, see Herbert Blau, "Readymade Desire."

2. *LONG DAY'S JOURNEY INTO NIGHT:*
THE SEEN AND THE UNSEEN

1. In Jamie's image, the front yard is an ocean, requiring a lighthouse by the front steps, one example of the fog's aqueous quality, by which Mary and Edmund seem so transformed.

2. For mention of the Shaughnessy episode, see, e.g., Floyd, 285; Barlow, 76–77; and Raleigh, 66. An exception to the rule of scant notice is Egil Tornqvist, who provides a lengthy discussion (241ff.). In it, he suggests that the story is a pattern for the play's lack of resolution. In Joel Pfister's analysis, the lines between Tyrone and Edmund in this scene are suggestive of O'Neill's ambivalent response to socialist politics.

3. Harker's name is similar to that of the hero of *More Stately Mansions*, Simon Harford, in whose play the capitalist end of the "American Dream" is fully explored and deconstructed. Simon's name also recalls "Harvard," divinity school to the U.S. theocracy. Barlow explains that in and around New London were the estates of two wealthy men O'Neill liked to satirize in his early poetry. Edward C. Hammond was the neighbor of James O'Neill's Irish tenant, John Dolan; and Edward S. Harkness was son to one of the founders of Standard Oil (112–13).

4. *Strange Interlude* in *Eugene O'Neill: Complete Plays, 1920–1931*. Further references to *Strange Interlude* and *The Hairy Ape* are from the Literary Classics edition and will be cited in the text.

5. Barlow finds that O'Neill thought of the play as a war and the family as a battlefield. Two of his proposed titles for the play were "The Long Day's

Insurrection" and "The Long Day's Retreat" (75). And Julia Kristeva, analyzing the images of the Virgin Mary in Catholic writings, says that she represents a "privileged *space*" (250–51; italics Kristeva's).

6. Others have compared Mary to Nina Leeds: Tiusanen, for example, suggests that Nina is Mary's prototype (223–24). See also Barlow (70), who follows Tiusanen's lead.

7. On Mary's centrality see Barlow, chap. 2; Chabrowe, 71; and Tiusanen, who makes the point implicitly by devoting to Mary much of his argument on *Long Day's Journey*.

8. Cf. Raleigh 24: "Fog also represents that blessed loss of identity for which all the main characters, the father excepted, are seeking." We will return to this theme in the discussion of *Iceman*.

9. The violent implications of this denial will be explored in chap. 5.

10. In Lionel Abel's classic theory of metatheatre, there is no modern tragedy, since tragedy requires the implacable values of a premodern age: "George Lukacs [sic] has said that the principal spectator of tragedy is God. I cannot imagine God present at a play of Shaw, Pirandello, or Genet. I cannot imagine Godot enjoying *Waiting for Godot*" (113).

11. The confusion—or conflation, rather—of remembering and forgetting seems not to have been lost on O'Neill. Two other possibilities for a title found scribbled in his notes were "What's Long Forgotten" and "What's [?] Long Unforgotten" (Barlow).

12. In a similar vein, Gerardine Meaney has argued that by refusing to play her maternal role, Mary represents a crisis of representability, at least until the final act.

13. Some elements of this chapter appear in " 'A Monster of Perfection': O'Neill's 'Stella.' " There I develop more fully the notion that Mary Tyrone is a threat to the play's Oedipal narrative logic.

3. THE ICEMAN COMETH: BUYING TIME

1. The belatedness of dramatic representation is demonstrated in Peter Brook's experiments with "Theatre of Cruelty." Invited to an evening of experimental theater, without advance explanation or program of any kind, the first night's audience gradually lost its sense of security in its role as spectator. At the second performance, however, the audience, knowing that the program had already been performed, reacted with more assurance. "The tension was no longer the same. . . . they knew we had already performed once before and the fact that there was nothing in the papers it-

self telegraphed a reassurance. The ultimate horrors could not have taken place" (Brook, 129–30). Whether or not "avant-garde" spectacle can be repeated is an interesting question brought up by the "retrospectives" of several avant-garde companies in New York City in the 1980s. Moreover, Brook insists that the "freedom" required to produce even avant-garde theater is itself achieved through rehearsal (repetition) (138).

2. Cf. Szondi; "According to Hegel, the Drama shows only that which the hero's subjectivity objectifies in action and that which this action retains of the objective world and transfers into subjectivity" (71).

3. *Strange Interlude*, act 8: "the only living life is in the past and future. . . . the present is an interlude . . . strange interlude in which we call on past and future to bear witness we are living!" (*Complete Plays* 784).

4. For some very different instances of this kind of criticism, see Austin Quigley; Richard Hornby; and Victor Turner, *The Anthropology of Performance*.

5. Artaud: "The Orphic Mysteries which subjugated Plato must have possessed on the moral and psychological level something of this definitive and transcendent aspect of the *alchemical theater*, with elements of an extraordinary psychological density, and conversely must have evoked the symbols of alchemy, which provide the spiritual means of decanting and transfusing matter, must have evoked the passionate and decisive transfusion of matter by mind" (52).

6. It's worth noting here that in act 3, when the characters are all testing their freedom, trying to become "real" by leaving the bar, there is a ritual returning of the keys to their rooms.

7. I borrow "the suspense of form" from Susanne K. Langer, who quotes Charles Morgan's point that " 'form in suspense' is the dramatic illusion itself, and the suspense of form something 'without which drama is not' " (311). Langer quotes from an essay titled "The Nature of Dramatic Illusion" published in 1933.

8. Aristotle says that tragedy originated as a single voice and developed toward dialogue, away from "satyric drama" (*On the Art of Poetry* 36–37). Nevertheless, the satyr play, "more closely related to the dance" than tragedy, remained as an appendage to it, a comic reflection on the tragic trilogy's serious theme. Commenting on Horace's discussion of the satyr play, editor T. S. Dorsch observes, "It is doubtful whether, as Horace suggests, the satyric drama came into being later than tragedy; the two forms seem rather to be different developments of the same origins" (86–87, n.3). Thus the tragedy was a dialogue that originated in monologue; and it was always

a double drama, including both a serious action and its comic, self-conscious double.

9. "Well before Baudelaire and Hoffmann, Friedrich Schlegel knew this very well when he defined irony, in a note from 1797, as '*eine permanente Parekbase.*' Parabasis is understood here as what is called in English criticism the 'self-conscious narrator,' the author's intrusion that disrupts the fictional illusion" (de Man 218–19).

10. "Irony is unrelieved *vertige*, dizziness to the point of madness. Sanity can exist only because we are willing to function within the conventions of duplicity and dissimulation, just as social language dissimulates the inherent violence of the actual relationships between human beings" (de Man 215–16).

11. After quoting Hebbel's point that bourgeois tragedy is based on the closure and confinement of individuals "incapable of dialectic" (Preface to *Maria Magdalena* [1844]), Szondi continues: " 'Closure' and the incapacity to engage in any (interpersonal) 'dialectic' destroyed the possibility of the Drama that had arisen from the decision of individuals to disclose themselves to one another. It did so at least as long as the 'most confined of spheres' did not force open this closure, as long as these isolated individuals, isolated although chained to one another, individuals whose discourse strikes wounds in the closure of another, were not forced to join in a second dialectic" (58). Szondi's translator, Michael Hays, notes that "[t]he manner in which Szondi plays with closure, disclosure, and decision here cannot be reproduced in English" (120 n.xv). And elsewhere Szondi analyzes Brecht's response to this "crisis" in the drama: "The increasingly problematic nature of interpersonal relationships calls the Drama itself into question, since dramatic form asserts that these relationships are unproblematic. This explains Brecht's attempt to oppose the Aristotelian theory and practice with a non-Aristotelian epic dramaturgy" (70).

12. In his essay "O'Neill's *Hairy Ape* and the Reversal of Hegelian Dialectics," Hubert Zapf shows that *The Hairy Ape* invokes a Marxist-Hegelian dialectical model, with its ideological implication of progress, which the play then "deconstructs."

13. I am indebted to Thomas Van Laan for the suggestion that Hickey "takes over" his play with monologue.

14. Judith Barlow, noting that O'Neill eliminated many references to Hickey's insanity in his final draft of the play, suggests that the playwright wanted to avoid the implication that Hickey is simply "mad" to begin with (see Liu and Swortzell 149–55). The notion of madness as a function of

history and in its relation to the social institution of "truth" is explored in chap. 5.

4. THE GLASS MENAGERIE: LOSS AND SPACE

1. Newman's *Glass Menagerie* was filmed in a Queens studio, and across the street the American Museum of the Moving Image later displayed the front room of his set, including examples of the retreated walls. The lighting effects were also recreated to show how the film established emotional and temporal atmosphere. Outside this exhibit, a monitor carried a continuous videotape of scenes from the film exhibiting these contrasts.

2. The notion of time as distance, the necessary relation between the awareness of time and the awareness of space—Einsteinian physics—is more important for an understanding of mimetic theory than it might at first seem. The psychological concept of time, Einstein suggests, might have originated in mimesis: in the disjuncture between experience and representation: "Of itself it is doubtful whether the differentiation between sense experience and recollection (or simple re-presentation) is something psychologically directly given to us" (139). The space between the empirical and the recapitulation of it only becomes evident in the attempt to bridge them. "Probably the ability to discriminate between these alternatives first comes about as the result of an activity of the mind creating order" (ibid.). Representation attempts to discriminate between events and the mind's ordering principle; by temporalizing events it repeats the mental process of differentiation that led to its analysis in the first place. Mimesis thus tries to create an understanding of the mind's ordering impulse by representing it. For a discussion of the influence of quantum theory on *The Glass Menagerie*, see Patricia C. Click.

3. James Reynolds has analyzed the play's concern with technology in "The Failure of Technology in *The Glass Menagerie*."

4. The curtain that produces secrecy and closure conceals the woman, partitions her and distances her. Curtaining effects become associated with the woman as she embodies the formal threat to formal order. Drapes, curtains, veils, and other mediations of the feminine serve not to shroud her in mystery but on the contrary to reveal her "mystery" as the revelation of the drama. This idea is more explicit in film, which, as Walter Benjamin says, "introduces us to unconscious optics as does psychoanalysis to unconscious impulses" (237). Film destroys the distance, the "aura" of the image, answering the masses' desire "to bring things 'closer' spatially and humanly" (223). The contemplation of the Madonna has been transformed

by the analysis of the image into a narrative of distinct, readable signs. Behind the destruction of distance lies a new "cult value" that relies on the image's remaining *hidden* and therefore open to the exposure of analysis (see Benjamin 225). This gender spacing, already explored in chapter 2, will be seen to have violent effects in *Streetcar* (chapter 5).

5. A photo of Tennessee Williams from 1947 (the year of *A Streetcar Named Desire*) taken by Eugene Smith shows Williams at the typewriter, hands folded meditatively around his cigarette holder, coffee and eyeglasses beside him. Three books lie in the foreground on his untidy desk: one has a plain black cover, one is Einstein's *Relativity*, and the other says, in large letters, *The Mysterious Universe*. The photograph looks extremely composed: an album of records is standing upright on the unmade bed, and we can see one of them playing on his phonograph; the books appear carelessly arranged, but all are turned toward the camera so that the bindings are exposed. Williams's introduction to *The Glass Menagerie* includes this comment on the uses of technology: "Our great technology is a God-given chance for adventure and for progress which we are afraid to attempt. Our ideas and our ideals remain exactly what they were and where they were three centuries ago. No. I beg your pardon. It is no longer safe for a man even to declare them!" (139). Williams will go on, as we have seen, to make the point (Scene 6) that only war mobilizes the possibilities inherent in mechanical reproduction. As Benjamin noted, society's "self-alienation has reached such a degree that it can experience its own destruction as an aesthetic pleasure of the first order. This is the situation of politics which Fascism is rendering aesthetic. Communism responds by politicizing art" (242; see also 241 and 251n.).

6. R. B. Parker, who has examined drafts of the play, finds in fact that the final version of *The Glass Menagerie* is a gentler play than the early drafts, which were "more sexually charged, more violent, and more blackly humorous"; "much more like what we have come to think of as typical Williams writing" (517–34).

5. *A STREETCAR NAMED DESIRE*:
SPATIAL VIOLATION AND SEXUAL VIOLENCE

1. I am indebted to my student Laurie Widdenstrom for this brilliant question. I isolate one underlying assumption of expressionism here—that of inner-outer space—in order to consider it as a formal point of comparison between expressionism and realism. The implications of invoking these two terms, however, and in such close association, are much broader.

As an avant-garde style in the literary and visual arts, expressionism was specifically antirealist and antinaturalist. As a political art it was also anti-materialist and antiscientific (anti-"objectivity"). Expressionism's politicization made it especially vulnerable to attack for its "subjectivity," detachment, and idealism. The Lukács-Bloch debate in *Das Wort* 1938 shows that, by the Popular Front period, expressionism's political position was crucial to its viability as a style; compared with realism it appeared "decadent," "immature," flimsy. "[B]ecause of the specifically anti-realist bias in Expressionism, . . . [the Expressionists] had no firm artistic hold on reality which might have corrected or neutralized their misconceptions. . . . [I]t intensified the dangers which inevitably accompany all such attempts to stabilize an essentially transitional ideology" (Lukács 51). Lukács's treatment of expressionism here is both ideological and dismissive; as a political movement it has for him simply "collapsed" (52). Texts on dramatic theory do not necessarily give the political resonance of expressionism more than a passing reference. Such concerns are often left to chapters on epic theater. The Lukács-Bloch arguments are reprinted in *Aesthetics and Politics*, however, and there is some discussion of the subject in both Levine chap. 2; and Vajda.

2. Compare Austin's realization, in *How to Do Things with Words* (148), that all language is "performative," that is, active and unpredictable, that it cannot simply be declarative, factual, "constative": "[T]he traditional 'statement' is an abstraction, an ideal, and so is its traditional truth or falsity" (ibid.).

3. What is repeated in the mimetic is, thus, something like the ongoing process of subjectivation as Lacan represents it. Subjectivation occurs through the rupture of the imaginary into the symbolic, where desire endlessly pursues the reparation of that rupture. As Judith Butler has shown, this means that the process of sexuation, too, is ongoing, continually failing, perhaps open to subversion. Lacan and Butler's ideas seem especially relevant to *Streetcar*. See my article "When a Door Is a Jar; or, Out in the Theatre: Tennessee Williams and Queer Space" for a discussion of *Streetcar* and queer vtheory.

4. William Kleb, too, suggests that in the final scene Blanche is transformed into a Foucauldian docile body. Others have noted the strain in the play's sense of closure. See June Schlueter, "We've had this date with each other from the beginning"; and Anca Vlasopolos.

5. The problem of literalizing and of localizing madness took on a new horror in medical practice in the United States during the thirties and forties, when psychosurgery became a relatively common means of tran-

quilizing those diagnosed with emotional disorders. Madness was seen to occupy the prefrontal lobes, and its cure was to sever them from the rest of the brain. The procedure, random and dangerous, was most often performed on patients in state institutions as a way of rendering them less violent and thus easier and cheaper to care for. Williams's sister Rose was one of many women in the United States who were lobotomized in this way. In his Memoirs Williams dates the lobotomy "in the early thirties" and recalls that Rose, who had been diagnosed with "dementia praecox," was removed from a Catholic sanatorium to the state asylum in Farmington, Missouri, in 1937 (Memoirs 158, 153). For a history of psychosurgery in the United States during this period, especially lobotomy, see Elliot S. Valenstein.

References

Abel, Lionel. *Metatheatre: A New View of Dramatic Form*. New York: Hill & Wang, 1963.

Aristotle. *On the Art of Poetry*. In *Classical Literary Criticism*. Trans. T. S. Dorsch. Harmondsworth, Middlesex: Penguin Books, 1965.

————. *The Politics*. Trans. T. A. Sinclair. Rev. Trevor J. Sunders. Harmondsworth, Middlesex: Penguin Books, 1981.

Artaud, Antonin. *The Theater and Its Double*. Trans. Mary Caroline Richards. New York: Grove Press, 1958.

Auerbach, Erich. *Mimesis: The Representation of Reality in Western Literature*. Trans. Willard J. Trask. Princeton: Princeton University Press, 1953.

Austin, J. L. *How to Do Things with Words*. 2d ed. Ed. J. O. Urmson and Maria Sbisa. Cambridge, Mass.: Harvard University Press, 1978.

Barlow, Judith E. *Final Acts: The Creation of Three Late O'Neill Plays*. Athens: University of Georgia Press, 1985.

Ben Chaim, Daphna. *Distance in the Theatre: The Aesthetics of Audience Response*. Ann Arbor: UMI Research Press, 1984.

Benjamin, Walter. *Illuminations*. Trans. Harry Zohn. Ed Hannah Arendt. New York: Schocken Books, 1969.

Bennett, Susan. *Theatre Audiences*. London: Routledge, 1990.

Bentley, Eric, ed. *The Theory of the Modern Stage*, Rev. ed. New York: Penguin Books, 1976.

Bernstein, Jeremy. *Einstein*. New York: Viking Press, 1973.

Blau, Herbert. *The Audience*. Baltimore: Johns Hopkins University Press, 1990.

————. *The Eye of Prey*. Bloomington: Indiana University Press, 1987.

————. "Readymade Desire." In *Confronting Tennessee Williams's "A Streetcar Named Desire": Essays in Critical Pluralism*. Ed. Philip C. Kolin. Westport, Conn.: Greenwood Press, 1993.

Brecht, Bertolt. *Brecht on Theatre*. Trans. and ed. John Willett. New York: Hill & Wang, 1964.

Brook, Peter. *The Empty Space*. New York: Atheneum, 1968.

Butler, Judith. "Imitation and Gender Insubordination." In *inside/out: Lesbian Theories, Gay Theories*. Ed. Diana Fuss. New York: Routledge, 1991.

Cargill, Oscar, Fagin, N. Bryllion, and Fisher, William J., eds. *O'Neill and His Plays: Four Decades of Criticism*. New York: New York University Press, 1961.

Carpenter, Frederic I. *Eugene O'Neill*. Revised ed. Boston: Twayne Publishers, 1979.

Chabrowe, Leonard. *Ritual and Pathos: The Theater of O'Neill*. Cranbury, N.J.: Associated University Presses, 1976.

Click, Patricia C. "The Uncertain Universe of *The Glass Menagerie*: The Influence of the New Physics on Tennessee Williams." *Journal of American Culture* 12:1 (Spring 1989), 41–45.

Clurman, Harold. *The Fervent Years: The Group Theatre and the Thirties*. New York: De Capo Press, 1975.

―――. Introduction. *Famous American Plays of the 1930's*. New York: Dell, 1968.

Derrida, Jacques. *Dissemination*. Trans. Barbara Johnson. Chicago: University of Chicago Press, 1981.

―――. *The Post Card*. Trans. Alan Bass. Chicago: University of Chicago Press, 1987.

―――. *Writing and Difference*. Trans. Alan Bass. Chicago: University of Chicago Press, 1978.

Diamond, Elin. "Mimesis, Mimicry, and the 'True-Real.'" *Modern Drama* 32:1 (March 1989), 58–72.

Einstein, Albert. *Relativity: The Special and the General Theory*. Trans. Robert W. Lawson. New York: Crown, 1961.

Eisen, Kurt. *The Inner Strength of Opposites: O'Neill's Novelistic Drama and the Melodramatic Imagination*. Athens: University of Georgia Press, 1994.

Eliot, T. S. *The Complete Poems and Plays, 1909–1950*. New York: Harcourt, Brace & World, 1971.

Esslin, Martin. *Antonin Artaud*. New York: Penguin Books, 1977.

Fergusson, Francis. *The Idea of a Theater*. Princeton: Princeton University Press, 1949.

Flanagan, Hallie. *Arena: The Story of the Federal Theatre*. 1940. Rpt. New York: Limelight Editions, 1985.

Fleche, Anne. "'A Monster of Perfection': O'Neill's 'Stella.'" In *Feminist Rereadings of Modern American Drama*. Ed. June Schlueter. Madison, N.J.: Fairleigh Dickinson University Press, 1989.

―――. "When a Door Is a Jar; or, Out in the Theatre: Tennessee Williams and Queer Space." *Theatre Journal* 47:2 (May 1995), 253–67.

Floyd, Virginia, ed. *Eugene O'Neill at Work: Newly Released Ideas for Plays*. New York: Frederick Ungar, 1981.

Foucault, Michel. *Discipline and Punish: The Birth of the Prison*. Trans. Alan Sheridan. New York: Vintage Books, 1979.

———. *The History of Sexuality*. Vol. 1. *An Introduction*. Trans. Robert Hurley. New York: Vintage Books, 1978.

———. *Madness and Civilization: A History of Insanity in the Age of Reason*. Trans. Richard Howard. New York: Vintage Books, 1965.

———. *Power/Knowledge: Selected Interviews and Other Writings, 1972–1977*. Ed. Colin Gordon. New York: Pantheon Books, 1980.

Gassner, John. *The Theatre in Our Times: A Survey of The Men, the Materials, and the Movements in the Modern Theatre*. New York: Crown Publishers, 1954.

Gombrich, E. H. *Art and Illusion: A Study in the Psychology of Pictorial Representation*. New York: Pantheon Books, 1960.

Hahn, Werner G. *Postwar Soviet Politics: The Fall of Zhdanov and the Defeat of Moderation, 1946–53*. Ithaca: Cornell University Press, 1982.

Himelstein, Morgan Y. *Drama Was a Weapon: The Left-Wing Theatre in New York, 1929–1941*. New Brunswick, N.J.: Rutgers University Press, 1963.

Hornby, Richard. *Drama, Metadrama, and Perception*. Lewisburg, Penn.: Bucknell University Press, 1986.

Kazan, Elia. *Elia Kazan: A Life*. New York: Alfred Knopf, 1988.

Kennedy, Adrienne. *Adrienne Kennedy in One Act*. Minneapolis: University of Minnesota Press, 1988.

Kleb, William. "Marginalia: Streetcar, Williams, and Foucault." In *Confronting Tennessee Williams's "A Streetcar Named Desire": Essays in Critical Pluralism*. Ed. Philip C. Kolin. Westport, Conn.: Greenwood Press, 1993.

Kristeva, Julia. *Desire in Language: A Semiotic Approach to Literature and Art*. Trans. Thomas Gora, Alice Jardine, and Leon S. Roudiez. Ed. Leon S. Roudiez. New York: Columbia University Press, 1980.

Kushner, Tony. *Angels in America, Part 1: Millennium Approaches*. New York: Theatre Communications Group, 1993.

———. *Angels in America, Part 2: Perestroika*. New York: Theatre Communications Group, 1994.

Lacan, Jacques. *Ecrits*. Trans. Alan Sheridan. New York: W. W. Norton, 1977.

Langer, Susanne K. *Feeling and Form*. New York: Charles Scribner's Sons, 1953.

de Lauretis, Teresa. *Alice Doesn't: Feminism, Semiotics, Cinema*. Bloomington: Indiana University Press, 1984.

Lawson, John Howard. *Theory and Technique of Playwriting*. New York: Hill & Wang, 1936.

Levin, Harry. "What is Realism?" *Comparative Literature* 3:3 (1951), 193–99.

Levine, Ira A. *Left-Wing Dramatic Theory in the American Theatre*. Ann Arbor: UMI Research Press, 1980.

Lindenberger, Herbert. "The Mimetic Bias in Modern Anglo-American Criticism." In *Mimesis in Contemporary Theory: An Interdisciplinary Approach*. Vol. 1. *The Literary and Philosophical Debate*. Ed. Mihai Spariousu. Philadelphia: John Benjamins, 1984.

Liu, Haiping, and Swortzell, Lowell, eds. *Eugene O'Neill in China: An International Centenary Celebration*. New York: Greenwood Press, 1992.

Lukács, Georg. "Realism in the Balance." In *Aesthetics and Politics*. New York: Verso, 1988.

Lyotard, Jean-François. *The Postmodern Condition: A Report on Knowledge*. Trans. Geoff Bennington and Brian Massumi. Minneapolis: University of Minnesota Press, 1984.

de Man, Paul. *Blindness and Insight: Essays in the Rhetoric of Contemporary Criticism*. 2d ed., rev. Minneapolis: University of Minnesota Press, 1983.

Mann, Bruce J. "An FBI Memorandum on O'Neill." *Eugene O'Neill Review* 15:1 (Spring 1991), 41–57.

Mathews, Jane De Hart. *The Federal Theatre, 1935–1939: Plays, Relief, and Politics*. Princeton: Princeton University Press, 1967.

Meaney, Gerardine. "*Long Day's Journey into Night*: Modernism, Postmodernism, and Maternal Loss." *Irish University Review: A Journal of Irish Studies* 21:2 (Fall–Winter 1991), 204–18.

Mielziner, Jo. *Designing for the Theatre*. New York: Bramhall House, 1965.

Nussbaum, Martha C. *The Fragility of Goodness: Luck and Ethics in Greek Tragedy and Philosophy*. New York: Cambridge University Press, 1986.

O'Neill, Eugene. *Complete Plays, 1920–1931*. New York: Literary Classics of the United States, 1988.

———. *The Iceman Cometh*. New York: Vintage Books, 1957.

———. *Long Day's Journey into Night*. New Haven: Yale University Press, 1955.

———. *Selected Letters of Eugene O'Neill*. Ed. Travis Bogard and Jackson R. Bryer. New Haven: Yale University Press, 1988.

Parker, R. B. "The Circle Closed: A Psychological Reading of *The Glass Menagerie* and *The Two Character Play*." *Modern Drama* 28 (December 1985): 517–34.

Pfister, Joel. *Staging Depth: Eugene O'Neill and the Politics of Psychological Discourse*. Chapel Hill: University of North Carolina Press, 1995.

Plato. *The Laws*. Trans. Trevor J. Saunders. Harmondsworth, Middlesex: Penguin Books, 1970.

———. *The Republic*. Trans. Desmond Lee. 2d ed., rev. London: Penguin Books, 1987.

―――. *Timaeus*. In *Timaeus and Critias*. Trans. Desmond Lee. Harmondsworth, Middlesex: Penguin Books, 1971.

Quigley, Austin. *The Modern Stage and Other Worlds*. New York: Methuen, 1985.

Ra'anan, Gavriel D. *International Policy Formation in the USSR*. Hamden, Conn.: Archon Books, 1983.

Rahv, Philip. "The Literary Class War." *New Masses* (August 1932), 7.

Raleigh, John Henry. *The Plays of Eugene O'Neill*. Carbondale: Southern Illinois University Press, 1965.

Reynolds, James. "The Failure of Technology in *The Glass Menagerie*." *Modern Drama* 34:4 (December 1991), 522–27.

Savran, David. *Communists, Cowboys, and Queers: The Politics of Masculinity in the Work of Arthur Miller and Tennessee Williams*. Minneapolis: University of Minnesota Press, 1992.

Schechner, Richard. *Performance Theory*. Rev. ed. New York: Routledge, 1988.

Schlueter, June. " 'We've had this date with each other from the beginning': Reading Toward Closure in *A Streetcar Named Desire*." In *Confronting Tennessee Williams's "A Streetcar Named Desire": Essays in Critical Pluralism*. Ed. Philip C. Kolin. Westport, Conn.: Greenwood Press, 1993.

Scolnikov, Hanna. "Mimesis, Mirror, Double." In *The Play Out of Context: Transferring Plays from Culture to Culture*. Ed. Hanna Scolnikov and Peter Holland. New York: Cambridge University Press, 1989.

Spariosu, Mihai, ed. *Mimesis in Contemporary Theory: An Interdisciplinary Approach*. Vol. 1. *The Literary and Philosophical Debate*. Philadelphia: John Benjamins, 1984.

Szondi, Peter. *Theory of the Modern Drama*. Trans. and ed. Michael Hays. Minneapolis: University of Minnesota Press, 1987.

Taylor, Ronald, translation ed. *Aesthetics and Politics*. New York: Verso, 1988.

Tiusanen, Timo. *O'Neill's Scenic Images*. Princeton: Princeton University Press, 1968.

Tornqvist, Egil. *A Drama of Souls: Studies in O'Neill's Super-naturalistic Technique*. Uppsala, Sweden: Almqvist & Wiksells, 1968.

Turner, Victor. *The Anthropology of Performance*. New York: Performing Arts Journal Press, 1986.

―――. *From Ritual to Theatre*. New York: Performing Arts Journal Press, 1982.

Vajda, György M. "Outline of the Philosophic Backgrounds of Expressionism." In *Expressionism as an International Literary Phenomenon*. Ed. Ulrich Weisstein. Budapest: Akademiai Kiadó, 1973.

Valenstein, Elliot S. *Great and Desperate Cures: The Rise and Decline of Psychosurgery* and Other Radical Treatments for Mental Illness. New York: Basic Books, 1986.

Vlasopolos, Anca. "Authorizing History: Victimization in A Streetcar Named Desire." Theatre Journal 38 (October 1986): 322–38.

Wiegand, Charmion von. "Playwright into Critic." New Theatre (April 1936), 35–36.

Wiles, Timothy J. The Theater Event: Modern Theories of Performance. Chicago: University of Chicago Press, 1980.

Williams, Jay. Stage Left. New York: Charles Scribner's Sons, 1974.

Williams, Tennessee. Collected Stories. New York: Ballantine Books, 1986.

———. The Glass Menagerie. In The Theatre of Tennessee Williams, vol. 1. New York: New Directions, 1971.

———. Memoirs. New York: Bantam Books, 1975.

———. The Night of the Iguana. In The Theatre of Tennessee Williams, vol. 4. New York: New Directions, 1972.

———. A Streetcar Named Desire. In The Theatre of Tennessee Williams, vol. 1. New York: New Directions, 1971.

———. "The Timeless World of a Play." In The Theatre of Tennessee Williams, vol. 2. New York: New Directions, 1971.

Zapf, Hubert. "O'Neill's Hairy Ape and the Reversal of Hegelian Dialectics." Modern Drama 31:1 (1988), 35–40.

Index

Abel, Lionel, 64; theory of "metatheatre," 118 (n. 10)

Albee, Edward, *Who's Afraid of Virginia Woolf?* 108

Allegory, 2, 99; and de Man's theory of irony, 50; de Man on, 91; and desire, 91–94

Aristotle, 19; and Brecht, 2; theory of art, 5–6, 9, 24, 115 (n. 17); compared to socialist realism, 11, 13–14; and Rahv's theory of catharsis, 11; and Brecht's theory of catharsis, 52–53; and tragedy, 13, 119–20 (n. 8); *On the Art of Poetry*, 14, 26, 52, 74, 77, 114 (n. 7), 119 (n. 8); theory of catharsis compared to *Iceman*, 52–53; on scale and proportion, 74, 87; compared to Langer's "virtual space," 74–76; and physics, 75; and plot duration, 77; and modern realism, 116 (n. 24)

Artaud, Antonin, 39, 41, 45; Derrida's reading of, 16–18; on character, 26; on language, 33–34, 68; on *alchemical theater*, 119 (n. 5)

Austin, J. L., *How to Do Things With Words*, 123 (n. 2)

Barlow, Judith, 117 (nn. 2, 3); *Final Acts*, 35; on Mary Tyrone, 35, 118 (nn. 6, 7); on titles for *Long Day's Journey*, 117–18 (nn. 5, 11); on Hickey's madness, 120 (n. 14)

Baudelaire, Charles, 120 (n. 10); theory of laughter, 61

Beckett, Samuel, compared to O'Neill, 46–47; *Waiting for Godot*, 118 (n. 10)

Ben Chaim, Daphna, *Distance in the Theatre*, 114 (n. 11)

Benjamin, Walter, on value of the image, 67, 70, 121–22 (n. 4); on fascism and technology, 81; on fascism and aesthetics, 122 (n. 5)

Bentham, Jeremy, 84, 86

Bernstein, Jeremy: on Aristotelian physics, 75; on "objective" time, 76–77

Black, Joel, "Idolology: The Model in Artistic Practice and Critical Theory," 115 (n. 20)

Blau, Herbert: *The Eye of Prey*, 114 (n. 9), 115 (n. 23); *The Audience*, 114 (n. 11); "Readymade Desire," 117 (n. 29)

Brecht, Bertolt, 74, 75, 92, 110, 120 (n. 11); and Aristotle, 2, 5–6, 67; on character, 26, 27; on epic, 49; on catharsis, 52–53; on film, 67, 81; on *Lehrstück*, 67; on emotion in epic, 69; *The Good Person of Setzuan*, 98

Brook, Peter, and "Theatre of Cruelty," 118–19 (n. 1)

Butler, Judith, 16, 17, 123 (n. 3)

Chekhov, Anton, 66, 67, 76, 77, 92

Citizen Kane, deep focus technique compared to *Glass Menagerie*, 71–72

Click, Patricia C., 121 (n. 2)

Clurman, Harold: *The Fervent Years*, 115 (n. 15); Introduction to *Famous American Plays of the 1930's*, 115 (n. 15)

Cohn, Roy, 110–11

de Lauretis, Teresa, and woman's relation to language, 33

de Man, Paul, 23, 43, 104; "The Rhetoric of Temporality," 50; on irony, 120 (n. 9); on irony and madness, 54, 60–62, 120 (n. 10); on irony and imitation, 61–62; on *The Fall*, 62–63; on allegory, 91–92; on desire, 93; on Lévi-Strauss's "virtual focus," 99–100

Derrida, Jacques, 115 (nn. 19, 20); Spariosu's criticism of, 6; theory of representation, 15; *Writing and Difference*, 16, 19, 24, 40, 77, 114 (n. 10); reading of Artaud, 16–18, 24; *Dissemination*, 16–17, 114 (n. 10); and Mallarmé's "Mimique," 16–17; and tragedy, 25, 41; on Foucault's

106; and heterosexuality, 90, 100; and allegory, 90–94, 98, 99, 101, 104, 106; as
realism, 93–96, 102–4, 106; as naturalism, 94; space and violence in, 94–99,
102–3; and relativity, 95–97, 105; as expressionism, 95–98, 101–3; and emotion, 96, 98; space and incest in, 97–
100; compared to Pirandellian
metatheater, 98; compared to Brecht, 98;
and madness, 100–106; space and madness in, 100–106, 123–24 (n. 5); and relation of madness to history, 103–6; and
temporality, 105–6; compared to *Iceman*,
106; space and gender, 121–22 (n. 4)

Szondi, Peter, 119 (n. 2); *Theory of the Modern Drama*, 27; on epic monologue, 59–
60; on epic montage, 69; on the "memory play," 82; on "dialectic" in the
drama, 120 (n. 11)

Turner, Victor, 116 (n. 23); *From Ritual to
Theatre*, 114 (n. 9); *The Anthropology of Performance*, 114 (n. 9), 119 (n. 4)

Tyrone, Mary, 27; relation to dialogue, 31–
34; compared to Nina Leeds, 31–33, 118
(n. 6); and acting, 31–32; as motivation

for dialogue, 32–34; materialized, 34;
difference from male characters, 34, 36,
42; and woman in modern drama, 34–
35; and structure of *Long Day's Journey*, 35–
36, 42; and change, 36, 41–42; and pres-
ence/absence, 42; lines compared to
Amanda Wingfield's, 77

Welles, Orson, 71

Wilde, Oscar, 5, 39, 113 (n. 5)

Williams, Rose Isabel, 124 (n. 5)

Williams, Tennessee: and realism, 1–2, 12–
15, 18–19, 44, 65–66, 107; *Night of the
Iguana*, 1–2; career compared to O'Neill's,
9–10, 21; and poststructuralism, 18–19,
21–23, 107–8; and Chekhov, 66, 67; *Portrait of a Madonna*, 70; "Desire and the
Black Masseur," 99, 106; compared to
Kushner, 110; as "Left-wing" writer,
117 (n. 28); *Memoirs*, 124 (n. 5). See also
Glass Menagerie; Streetcar Named Desire

Wilson, Lanford, *The Rimers of Eldritch*, 108

Zapf, Hubert, 120 (n. 12)

Zhdanovschina, 115 (n. 16)

About the Author

Anne Fleche is Assistant Professor of English at Boston College. She received her master's and doctorate degrees from Rutgers University. Her other publications include chapters in *Feminist Re-readings of Modern American Drama* (1989), edited by June Schulueter, and *"May All Your Fences Have Gates": Essays on the Drama of August Wilson* (1994), edited by Alan Nadel, as well as articles in *Modern Drama* and *Theatre Journal*.

3